God is moving in unprecedented ways t[...] of reaching the nations, though it is not [...] sacrifice on the part of those who dare to be obedient to his call. This gripping testimony of a family willing to go to the ends of the earth is filled with emotion and intrigue. Another stronghold of Satan crumbles and God is glorified as a family walks through the tragedy of a modern-day martyrdom. Every reader will be challenged to abandon a comfortable, self-centered lifestyle for a deeper devotion to showing Christ's love for a lost world.

JERRY RANKIN
President Emeritus of International Mission Board, SBC

Ten days before the tragic event described in this book, an African colleague and I had dinner at Emily and Stephen's home. When I asked Stephen how he was dealing with the risks of speaking boldly about Isa al Masih (Jesus) in this challenging place, he smiled. "A few months ago I sensed God inviting me to seize more opportunities to speak openly with people and occasionally give away Bibles," he said. "And I have done that as God led me. A few years back, when Emily and I were still learning Arabic and French, we made a decision. You see, we died before we came here!" Years later, tears come to my eyes almost every time I try to share what Stephen said. And now, with this wonderful book, Emily has invited all of us into her family's remarkable journey of high intentionality in proclaiming the kingdom of God where Jesus is about to go.

JERRY TROUSDALE
Author of *Miraculous Movements: How Hundreds of Thousands of Muslims Are Falling in Love with Jesus* and director of International Ministries at Cityteam Ministries

I personally walked the streets of the capital of the desert country where Stephen and Emily Foreman served. As you, too, walk through these pages, seeing the tragedy that is turning to triumph, the book will not just tug at your heart; it will break your heart—and then you will see that resurrection comes after death in Christ alone. As you read, you will find your own heart changed, and you will grow in maturity through seeing the experiences of this family serving in one of the neediest areas of the world. This book is written by one of my true heroes. And it's authentic because it's real life after death.

LOREN CUNNINGHAM
Founder of Youth with a Mission (YWAM)

We died before we came here

A TRUE STORY OF SACRIFICE AND HOPE

EMILY FOREMAN

A NavPress resource published in alliance
with Tyndale House Publishers, Inc.

NavPress is the publishing ministry of The Navigators, an international Christian organization and leader in personal spiritual development. NavPress is committed to helping people grow spiritually and enjoy lives of meaning and hope through personal and group resources that are biblically rooted, culturally relevant, and highly practical.

For more information, visit www.NavPress.com.

We Died Before We Came Here: A True Story of Sacrifice and Hope

Copyright © 2016 by J. Stanley. All rights reserved.

A NavPress resource published in alliance with Tyndale House Publishers, Inc.

NAVPRESS and the NAVPRESS logo are registered trademarks of NavPress, The Navigators, Colorado Springs, CO. *TYNDALE* is a registered trademark of Tyndale House Publishers, Inc. Absence of ® in connection with marks of NavPress or other parties does not indicate an absence of registration of those marks.

Cover watercolor cross copyright © Prixel Creative/Lightstock. All rights reserved.

Cover and interior photograph of shadow by lulu and isabelle/Creative Market. All rights reserved.

Cover and interior photograph of entry and columns by cineuno/Creative Market. All rights reserved.

Cover and interior photograph of oasis copyright © Anthon Jackson/Stocksy. All rights reserved.

Published in association with The Blythe Daniel Agency, Inc., PO Box 64197, Colorado Springs, CO 80962.

The Team:
Don Pape, Publisher
Caitlyn Carlson, Acquiring Editor, Development Editor
Jennifer Ghionzoli, Designer

All Scripture quotations, unless otherwise indicated, are taken from the Holy Bible, *New International Version,*® *NIV.*® Copyright © 1973, 1978, 1984, 2011 by Biblica, Inc.® Used by permission. All rights reserved worldwide.

Scripture quotations marked KJV are taken from the *Holy Bible*, King James Version.

Scripture quotations marked NASB are taken from the New American Standard Bible,® copyright © 1960, 1962, 1963, 1968, 1971, 1972, 1973, 1975, 1977, 1995 by The Lockman Foundation. Used by permission.

Scripture quotations marked NKJV are taken from the New King James Version,® copyright © 1982 by Thomas Nelson, Inc. Used by permission. All rights reserved.

Scripture quotations marked NLT are taken from the *Holy Bible*, New Living Translation, copyright © 1996, 2004, 2015 by Tyndale House Foundation. Used by permission of Tyndale House Publishers, Inc., Carol Stream, Illinois 60188. All rights reserved.

To protect the identities of those involved, all names have been changed throughout this book.

Cataloging-in-Publication Data is available.

ISBN 978-1-63146-451-5

Printed in the United States of America

22   21   20   19
7   6   5   4

For my precious children: Heidi, Joshua, Ellie, and Piper.
What a journey we've been on, and what a gift to walk it with
you! Thank you for graciously accepting the plans God has had
for our family and for bringing so much joy to our journey
even when we faced hardships. Thank you for making life on
mission fun. I'm so proud to be your mother. Not only do I see
so much of your dad in each of you, but I also see a reflection of
your heavenly Father, who has given you purpose and hope.

CONTENTS

INTRODUCTION

THIS BOOK IS A TRUE STORY of real people and real places. Although names have been changed to protect the workers and the ongoing work in North Africa, this hasn't been done out of fear or a desire for safety. I absolutely believe that every true follower of Christ should be willing to give his or her life for Jesus' sake and his purposes, but to do so for the sake of a book would be a waste of precious life.

Writing this book has been an extremely vulnerable experience for me. I was against the idea in the beginning. Though my journey with the Lord has been a rich one full of blessing, I just wasn't sure I wanted to relive the most difficult and painful parts of my life. Eventually, I felt prompted by the Holy Spirit to give an account of our experiences and ultimately of God's faithfulness. My family has learned much about the nature and character of God through scary and uncertain times living in a 100 percent Muslim country—and also through the fun, exciting, and blessed times of discovering the beauty behind the facade of the Islamic reputation. Through ups and downs, sickness and health, dangers and security, the sum of our experiences recounted in this book is God's faithfulness.

I hope this story will shed light on the realities of taking the risk of living cross-culturally as a family in an Islamic context. And I hope the reader will find faith and inspiration through my family's journey—and perhaps even find some wisdom in "what not to do." It was a seven-year learning curve for us to grow in our understanding of what goes on in the minds of our Muslim friends. Most of all, I want the truth to be told—truth that culture and our Western fears have modified for the sake of safety. May God break our hearts for those his heart breaks for.

Emily Foreman

the butcher

THE OLD GATED mosque stood deserted, its beautiful slender minaret piercing the vast blue desert sky. The faithful followers who had come to the mosque for their early morning prayers had returned home. As the wind picked up, dust began rolling in from the distant dunes, creating whirlwinds of trash from the market street. Most of the businesses were quiet—no one had yet opened the doors of their clothing boutiques or set up their phone-credit stands. All was quiet except for the sounds of rusty old taxis in the distance and the barking of stray dogs. A few goats moseyed about the mostly empty dirt streets, picking through the trash for something edible.

As usual, the butcher was one of the few people out this time of day. After the morning call to prayer, he had gone straight to his stand and began sorting through the bloody, fly-covered carcasses of the two goats he had slaughtered earlier. He hoped it would be Allah's will that he'd sell enough meat to provide for his wife and five children today.

As he began sharpening his carving knife, the butcher absently noticed the lone red car still parked on the other side of the dirt street. It had been there since dawn, when everyone had come for prayers.

He heard the familiar rumbling of a truck as it pulled up outside the training center across the street. The tall American, Stephen Foreman, climbed out and walked around to the passenger door to retrieve his things. He greeted the butcher with his usual friendly grin, shouting, "*As-salamu alaikum!*" across the street.

The butcher was always struck by the kindness of this American, who treated him with as much respect as he did those of the upper class. He smiled back and waved. "*Wa-alaikum asalam!*"

It was 8:20 a.m. Stephen was always early, the first to arrive at the center.

The doors on the red car opened. Two young men emerged and walked toward Stephen. The butcher paused as the three began talking back and forth, their voices getting louder, the conversation becoming heated.

Then the two young men grabbed the American by the arms and tried to pull him toward their car.

Stephen resisted and overpowered the first man, holding him to the ground with his foot while struggling with the second man. Another man emerged from the red car to help in the attempt to overcome the American.

The butcher saw the danger and began to run to Stephen's aid—but before he could take three steps he stopped, frozen in his tracks by the sound echoing between the cement walls of the mosque and the training center.

POP! POP! POP!

CHAPTER 1

the Prison

SEVEN YEARS EARLIER

THE PRISON COMPOUND squatted on a dismal, dusty street a distance from the main paved road. We pulled up outside a crumbling, gray cement wall. The prison guards let us in through a large metal door and led us across a grungy cement courtyard toward the entrance of what had originally been an old house. A small shack with what seemed to be the only window in the place stood at one end of the courtyard, and inside guards were lying about on thin mats on the floor, watching an old dusty TV and drinking hot mint tea out of a shared shot glass. A rusty steel-barred gate creaked in welcome as we stepped nervously into the main building.

Nothing in my past experience prepared me for this

prison. I had seen heart-wrenching documentaries on life in US prisons, but nothing, save the documentaries on concentration camps during World War II that we were forced to watch in high school, could compare to what we would encounter in the prisons of this country in North Africa.

We were spending five weeks in this desert land, working with an NGO as part of the practical phase of the missions school we had been training with for six months. We believed this would be good preparation for a call to long-term missions somewhere. My husband, Stephen—accompanied by our four-year-old son, Joshua—worked every day in the ferocious sun, building a home for a mother of nine whose makeshift shack had collapsed. I and some other women on our team—as well as my three-year-old and six-year-old daughters—were working at a women's prison.

We wondered who and what we would encounter. What were these women in prison for? Were they dangerous, hardened criminals?

Evidently the inmates had heard we were coming. They were not confined to cells as we'd imagined, but were grouped in a communal living area. As soon as they saw us they started clapping, singing, and dancing in excitement. In true hospitable African fashion, they wanted to celebrate the arrival of their unusual visitors.

But the celebrations were quickly cut short. As we watched in horror, the guards got their whips out and began thrashing the women to shut them up.

I quickly tucked my girls behind me, trying to shield them

from what was happening. I whispered under my breath, "Oh God! What have I gotten myself into? What have I gotten my babies into?"

We were probably not the people you'd expect to be doing this, Stephen and I. Sure, we'd started out starry-eyed and full of passion. I'd been that kid who was determined to tell all my friends about Jesus and who couldn't sleep the night after a missionary doctor had told our church stories about children in Africa. Stephen had gone on a mission trip to Mexico in high school and heard God whisper, *This is what I have for you.*

But when we met, I was a part-time college student working three part-time jobs, trying to support myself and wrap my head around being a single mom. During the four years my ex-boyfriend and I dated, I allowed my relationship with God to fade—at least until the wake-up call the day I took the pregnancy test. I was immediately broken and longed to make my life right again. Not only for my sake, but for the child's. My boyfriend wasn't interested in my renewed relationship with God—and he definitely wasn't interested in marriage and raising our child together. So there I was, alone and certain I had lost my right to dream of a relationship with a man who would love me and my child and have an all-consuming, red-hot zeal to glorify God.

At the same time, Stephen was facing the death of his first marriage—and of his dreams of serving God on the mission field. He and his wife had married right out of college, full of plans to serve God anywhere he would lead them. But as they started their missionary training, she pulled the plug on their dreams, deciding she wasn't comfortable with a life of what she called "begging" for the financial support to go. And Stephen accepted it. He wanted nothing more than to keep his marriage together. But despite his efforts, they began to drift apart, and she eventually filed for divorce.

Stephen had caught my eye at church camp a decade earlier, but I'd never even known his name. He was the manager at one of my part-time jobs, and in the midst of our individual dream-dashing moments, we became friends. I was sure it would be nothing more than that—I was pregnant, after all. But as the months passed, we both sensed it—we were falling in love. Stephen's acceptance of my situation, and his unconditional, fatherly love for this child I was carrying, was one of the most incredible expressions of God's provision and faithfulness I would ever experience. And not only were we being redeemed from our individual places of devastation—we were also being drawn into a united life of restoration.

Even so, we both felt that the call we'd heard from God was fraught with obstacles from the start. Would a divorced man be allowed to become a leader in the church or in service overseas? Would a young woman who'd become pregnant out of wedlock be permitted to go?

But God, of course, was not troubled by our pasts. He kept bringing to my mind the adulterous woman in the

Bible, waiting for Jesus' response as the crowd hovered over her with stones. As Jesus stooped down, he didn't reach for a stone but began to write in the dirt. For Stephen and me, the ground was our hearts, and Jesus was beginning—or, rather, continuing—to write his story. Not a story of condemnation, but a story of redemption.

Shortly after we started dating, Stephen handed me *Foxe's Book of Martyrs*, a daunting volume that chronicles the persecution and suffering of Christians throughout the centuries, starting with the biblical account of the apostle Stephen. "I feel it is only fair that you understand my level of commitment to God and his call on my life to take the gospel to the ends of the earth," he told me, an unusually serious look on his face. "No matter the cost."

As I read the stories of martyr after martyr, I felt overwhelmed as I attempted to calculate that cost. Was I really that serious about following Jesus? What would I have to give up to do this? How far would I be willing to go with God? What would I do if I were in a situation of choosing whether to deny Christ and live, or refuse to deny him and die? Was I willing to give my life for Christ? Was I willing to support Stephen's willingness to give his life for Christ?

Stephen's *yes* was already on the table. Was mine?

Five years into our marriage, with three very young kids and Stephen now heading up a branch of a large supply company in our town with great job prospects ahead, I could no longer avoid the question. In our marriage we were dedicated to loving God and loving others, not just in word but in deed. But as this passion had grown, so had the agitation in our spirits—a sense of holy discontent. The comfortable was becoming increasingly uncomfortable. The two great commands had to be linked to the great commission in a more concrete way. It was not, after all, the "great suggestion." God's hand beckoned to the unknown—an adventure of faith. Stephen and I had a tough choice, and yet, in the mystery of God's sovereignty, we didn't. We began to burn with an intense desire to do the impossible. We needed to "go." We didn't know where. We only knew it had to be somewhere difficult because all of the easy places were taken. There were far too many people in the world who had never heard that God had provided a way to him through his Son, Jesus Christ. Stephen often quoted a phrase in church and youth group, which his own youth leader had used to inspire him and his peers: "If not you, who? If not now, when?"

As we shared our burden for overseas ministry with our church leadership and close friends, many of them, with good intentions, tried to help us be more logical. "But there is so much need right here at home!" they would argue. "And anyway, it's too dangerous to go trekking across the world with such small children!"

Despite their most sincere efforts to convince us to be reasonable, we couldn't shake God's call on our hearts. We kept thinking about Oswald J. Smith's words: "No one has the right to hear the gospel twice, while there remains someone who has not heard it once."

And yet now, standing in this prison, all I wanted to do was flee back to the airport. God's mission for us here was to tell captives about his true freedom—but how was this going to impact my children? My heart was in conflict. A "good mother" wouldn't subject her children to this.

But a "good daughter" to the heavenly Father would.

About forty women were housed haphazardly in the communal prison quarters, all sharing the three small rooms that led off the commons. Everything was extremely dirty, and the walls were in serious need of a coat of paint. We saw a few rats, and roaches were everywhere—on the floor, in the walls, and in the mats where the women slept. But the women seemed completely oblivious to the rodents and pests.

There were only two women working with us who could occasionally help interpret, so for the most part we were left to our own devices. We did our best with made-up sign language. The women seemed so excited that we were there and anxious for outside attention that they didn't mind the lack of verbal communication.

We learned many of their stories through the translator. Many of the women were imprisoned for the crime of *Zina*—sexual misconduct. Shockingly, a few of them had been imprisoned because they'd been raped. In this society, where women had very few rights, a woman took the blame for sexual relations outside of marriage, whether she'd been involved willingly or not. An illegitimate pregnancy sealed her guilt. According to sharia law, pregnancy could only be achieved through a consensual act, so the woman could make no defense.

A few of the women in the prison had been impregnated by the guards. While some were angry and sensed the injustice, most seemed resigned to their fate, believing it was "Allah's will." Other women seemed to care little about their own dignity and would even sell their bodies to the guards in exchange for cigarettes or sweets.

A couple of the women were in prison for drug dealing. One rich, upper-class woman had murdered her husband. By law, it was up to the closest male relative to decide how long she would stay in prison. Her closest male relative was her son, who wouldn't get to make the decision until he turned eighteen. If he forgave her, she would be set free. But if he chose not to, she would remain in prison for life.

The whole judicial system seemed so screwed up. If a woman had connections, she could simply pay her way out even if she was actually guilty of a crime, but many others in the prison seemed to be held unjustly. They might be locked up for several years before their cases would be heard. Because of the culture of shame and honor, their families would often disown them, leaving them with no resources for a lawyer.

The guards, all of them men, treated the women very harshly. Their whips came out at the slightest provocation. If two women argued, they'd be shackled at the ankles in the courtyard and weren't allowed to participate in our activities.

How could we show these women God's love—especially

in a land where our faith was forbidden? We couldn't do much spiritual work in the prison for fear of harming the long-term ministry in the country. So instead of obvious evangelism or church planting, we ministered in the quiet, patient work of building relationships. A few of us volunteered to help with sewing classes that were being run in the prison. I'd taken home-economics classes at school and had quilted with my grandmother—that was as far as my skills went. But I knew that whatever I had, God could use.

In one of our last weeks of short-term ministry in the country, we experienced our first sandstorm. While it was reportedly a mild storm (lasting "only" a few days), we felt like we were under house arrest. The sun was a ten-watt light bulb in the sky, hidden behind a haze of dust.

When the water reservoir at our team house began to dry up, we began to feel the muted panic of providing for our family in this desert land. I started compulsively counting down the days till we could leave. *Four more weeks, God. I can't make it!*

Two more days . . . I can't make it!

After five weeks in the desert, I was ready to get back to some air-conditioning and cookie-dough Blizzards.

One more day, God. I can't make it . . .

Before we had come here, I had laid my *yes* on the table. *Wherever you want us to go, God.* Wasn't that all I had to do? But now, here, with my babies in this hot and sandy great unknown, I was extremely uncomfortable. Was this what Paul meant by "dying daily"?

As I prayed, the Lord gave me a glimpse into my own heart. What I saw made me even more uncomfortable. What I had considered "courage" in leaving everything to serve him was really just pride. I had even fooled myself. I had loved the identity of being radical and being willing to do something that few even dared. In his loving sovereignty God also showed me what was behind me, that the door I had stepped through to set out on this incredible adventure was still standing open. I had an out. If I chose to turn back, he would still love me and even use me.

I had a choice to make. The door behind opened to a short path leading to a shiny new minivan and a comfortable three-bedroom house and white picket fence. It was a lovely path with perfectly shaped stepping-stones of self-preservation. And the door ahead? That door opened to a narrow, scary, and uncertain yet far more fulfilling and purpose-filled path that didn't end—it led all the way into eternity. I didn't have the courage it would take, nor the strength. But God assured me that my own courage and strength is not what he wants. He wants only my willingness.

If I called you back here, would you come?

The five weeks were finally over. We were on our way out. I was on cloud nine.

But then, on that last day, our team leader, Lucia, decided

to give us one last tour of the entire city. My joy sank underneath the reality we encountered. The weight of the need in this land was as clear as day.

As we passed through downtown, everything looked old and dirty—the cars, the buildings, the people. We were still in disbelief at the madness of third-world traffic: trucks with only the suggestion of previous paint; minibuses without bumpers; battered cars with duct tape for windows; donkey carts and bicycles; buses with people hanging out the windows, tightly clutching their sacks and baskets; pedestrians making the life-risking dash across six-way traffic in a four-lane intersection. Traffic signals were optional. Stop signs were mere suggestions. Everybody made up his or her own rules of where and when to drive, and right of way came down to who was the bravest.

More difficult than dodging other vehicles and pedestrians was dodging the swarm of beggars. Some were in wheelchairs. Others crawled or pulled their shriveled bodies—little more than skin and bone—along the dirty ground, trying to shield their hands or knees with worn out, mismatched flip flops. I had been exposed to some poverty on church trips to Mexico, but this was on another level entirely.

Boys ranging from the ages of three to sixteen or seventeen would spend all day standing on the burning pavement, holding out their large empty tomato-paste cans and begging at car windows. Most of them, Lucia explained, were sent by their poor families in distant villages to the imam—the holy man—to learn the Qur'an. Usually the families had no idea the desperate situation they'd sent their children into. The boys spent only an hour or so each day memorizing the Qur'an with the teacher before being sent out to beg for the rest of the day. If they didn't meet their quotas by the end of the day, they were beaten or left outside for the night. Sometimes a car would hit one of the boys and no one would come to identify him. Other times, boys would just disappear—possibly into the dark realm of human trafficking. My throat tightened as I looked at their malnourished bodies, callused feet, and hopeless faces smeared with dirt and sweat.

Those faces lingered in my mind as we arrived at the airport two hours before our flight, or so we thought. By 2:00 a.m. we were still waiting for our rustic North African airline to grace us with its presence. I was about ready to curl up on the dirty, sand-colored tile floor. But because all three kids had decided to sprawl themselves over me, I couldn't move. I didn't know why they weren't lying on Stephen—he had a lot more cushioning, though he had lost a bit of weight during the strenuous outreach.

Had it really been only five weeks? It felt like five months. All of us were well and truly spent. How could anyone get used to life in the desert?

The images from earlier that day rolled over and over in my restless mind. The need in this place was overwhelming. I felt hopeless as I thought about the poor we'd seen and tried to reconcile the abject poverty I had witnessed with the overabundance of comfort I was now headed back to.

Suddenly I sensed a prompting in my spirit.

If I called you back here, would you come?

Really, God? You're asking me that now? Perhaps if I tried hard enough, I could fall asleep sitting up and not have to answer.

But the quiet question persisted.

Will you come back here? Are you willing to truly trust me with your life, your children, and your future?

I looked down at little Joshua, stroking the hair from his closed eyes. *God sacrificed his own Son for me and my children. Will I not trust him with their lives, our future?*

I was tired of the struggle in my heart. I prayed for deeper faith and trust and exhaled slowly. *Yes, Lord. I surrender. Again.* And I prayed for grace to face the daily inevitabilities—the temptation to back out, to play it safe, to escape death. Day after day I would once again have to "die" to that, to myself, to my right to have full control over my family's life.

After we'd all finally settled into our seats on the plane, I glanced at Stephen. He seemed lost in deep thought, and exhaustion was written all over his face. He looked as though he'd just walked off a battlefield.

He stared out the window as we took off. The sparse lights of the city disappeared as our plane ascended.

"You look a million miles away," I observed. "What're you thinking?"

He looked over at me, his expression both amused and concerned. "You might not want to hear this."

"Well, you're gonna have to tell me now."

He looked down at Ellie, who was lying peacefully across

his lap, then back up at me. "While we were waiting in the airport, God asked me if I'd be willing to come back here . . . long term. If he called us back . . ."

I let out a laugh. "God was asking me the same thing! I thought you were sleeping."

"God works in mysterious ways." Stephen chuckled. "I admit, the outreach wasn't a bed of roses, and I didn't exactly love the country. I know you and the kids didn't have the easiest time either."

"I was counting down the days."

Stephen sighed. "I know . . . but I told God we'd go wherever he asks us to."

As I stared out into the night sky, I thought, *Well, Lord, this was just a test, right? You just wanted to make sure our hearts were right. You're really gonna send us somewhere easier . . .*

CHAPTER 2

The Dangerous Prayer

"**BREAK MY HEART, GOD. BREAK MY HEART** with the things that break your heart."

It's a dangerous prayer to pray.

I'd always had a clear understanding that people needed the gospel, but having seen that need firsthand, I was overwhelmed by the enormity of the task. I wanted to go everywhere, tell everyone about the love and sacrifice of Christ, meet every need—but I couldn't. I was one tiny human being on a globe full of lost and broken people. Yet I knew that God had a purpose for my life, for my marriage, and for my family.

After we'd returned to the States, I'd decided to enroll in a course on cross-cultural ministry. Stephen joined our ministry organization in the admissions department, where his administrative skills would be put to good use. A few weeks into school, a man from The Navigators came to share with us about reaching out to the Muslim world. I wished I could have heard this man before our outreach in North Africa. As he talked about the beliefs and world-view of Muslims, the things I had seen and heard in the women's prison started to make sense. As he went on to explain the values of Muslim society and the struggles of Muslim women, I couldn't take notes fast enough. God was answering my prayer with a crushing conviction. As I felt his heart breaking over these women, my heart broke too. I sensed that he had been preparing my "soul soil" during those weeks in the women's prison. I'd been given a snapshot of Muslim women all over the world suffering injustice at the hands of Islamic patriarchal society. All of them were in a prison of some form—physical, mental, spiritual, or all three. And because of their fatalistic view of Allah's will, they had little hope even of seeing the injustice for what it was.

My passion was ignited. I had finally found my purpose.

As I shared my revelation with Stephen that evening, a broad grin spread across his face. "I know we've been praying together about it, but what I didn't tell you is that God's been speaking pretty loud and clear to me for a while now," he said, excitement seeping out through his voice. "I just wanted you to hear from the Lord yourself so I wouldn't be the one putting ideas in your head."

"Oh yeah? And what ideas would those be?" I gave him a puzzled smile.

"Well, I've known we're called to minister to Muslims, ever since we went to North Africa. I even told one of the leaders about it while we were there."

I prodded Stephen playfully. "So much for marital transparency, huh?" But neither of us could stop smiling. God had answered our prayers. But where exactly would he point the compass?

The country in North Africa where God first introduced me to the need of Muslim women was at the very bottom of my list of possibilities. It had been so hard, so overwhelming, and it had very little to offer my children—and besides, people need to hear about Jesus in other, more developed Muslim countries too, right? Within the next few months we'd narrowed down our target destination to somewhere else in the vicinity of North Africa or the Middle East. Where would be the best place for a family with small children? *God wouldn't send us somewhere we couldn't push a stroller, surely,* I told myself.

We were anxious to get our plans in place, so, scrambling for new ideas, we emailed the North Africa regional directors for our training company and explained our desire to be placed where our experience and credentials would be most useful. We were convinced that if we simply made ourselves available, the Lord would place us where he wanted us.

We received a reply within minutes. "Have you considered the country in North Africa where you were recently?"

We looked at each other.

"You realize this is risky business, right?" I asked Stephen.

"Yes," he said with a slow nod. "I've given that a lot of thought and prayer. The Lord keeps bringing me back to Galatians 2:20, and I've come to the conclusion that if we've already died to ourselves, and the life we have in Christ now is eternal, then ultimately what is there to lose?"

It was suddenly so clear—this was the place God had had in mind all along. He'd gotten us both to acknowledge it while we were there, and we'd explained it away, vainly trying to find our own alternative. As the truth sunk in, I felt God's absolute peace descend on my heart. We didn't have to think about it very long. Five minutes later, we sent our reply. Another *yes* laid on the table.

The doors started opening immediately. Lucia, our fearless team leader who headed up an NGO in the country, was planning to go home to Brazil to study law. With Stephen's business administration background, he fit the open post of NGO director perfectly. Within a week, we had the go-ahead. This whirlwind brought us relief and immense excitement. We would aim to be in North Africa by July of the following year.

We knew that God had called us to go where very few would go, and we were aware of the risks we'd have to face. From the beginning we counted the cost. We knew that Muslims could potentially be extremist and hostile to anything that smelled of Christianity. We'd read plenty of stories of Christians being martyred and persecuted. Recently an American family working with an organization in North Africa had faced such a crisis. A man who had been drinking approached their vehicle, pointed a gun through the window, and pulled the trigger. The bullet grazed the father's arm and went into his daughter's chest. Fortunately, she'd survived and the family was immediately evacuated to a hospital in Europe. Sometimes I wished we hadn't heard the stories. These things replayed constantly in our minds, and we had to keep giving our anxieties over to God.

We also understood that "safety" was not a New Testament concept but merely an American one. Jesus never called his disciples to safety but rather to obedience. He didn't say, "Lay down your cross, relax, and be comfortable" or "I'm sending you out as sheep among sheep." Rather, he said, "Take up your cross, and follow me" (Matthew 16:24, NLT) and "I am sending you out as sheep among wolves" (10:16, NLT). And the ultimate promise that would make the scariest venture possible: "And surely I am with you always, to the very end of the age" (28:20, NLT). He never denied that hardship would be part of the bargain. But he also promised there would be great joy and peace in following him. Ultimately, it boiled down to one thing: Was he truly worthy of our lives? And there was no debating that.

I had no doubts about my willingness to lay my own life down. But my children's safety was another subject entirely. How could I find the balance between common sense and faith? What about my responsibility as their mother? Or was it just plain fear I was struggling with? It was going to be a daily battle to stand firm against fear. But if Stephen ever felt any fear, he didn't show it. While he also had deep concerns for our children's well-being, he never let his concern turn into full-blown fear or discouragement. He was a constant source of positivity, and whenever I came to him with doubts, he would just keep reminding me that God is God. I was thankful for that—and thankful that Stephen was Stephen.

It was one of my rare mornings to sleep in. We now had another newborn—Piper, our third daughter—and my mother-in-law had offered to get up with her that day. We were staying with Stephen's parents before heading off to Quebec for French language training, our final step before leaving for North Africa.

When I finally traipsed down the stairs, still a little groggy, I noticed that the house seemed unusually quiet. All I could hear were the faint sounds of the TV. I ventured into the TV room to find my father-in-law leaning forward in his recliner, the rest of the family huddled around his chair back, all eyes glued to the screen.

"What's going on?" I asked.

Stephen's father answered without turning his head, his voice sounding distant. "The beginning of World War Three . . ."

Stephen was a little pale. "A plane just crashed into one of the World Trade Center towers."

"You're kidding, right?" I hurried over to join the huddle.

Sure enough, footage replayed of a Boeing 767 slamming into the North Tower. We sat and watched, speechless, as smoke and ash spewed from a gaping wound in the building's side. We were so confused. How had the plane gotten so off course? There had to be an explanation.

Then suddenly, as we watched, a second plane tore into the South Tower. Shock and fear swallowed that early confusion as both towers collapsed before our eyes like a pair of accordions squeezed down by an invisible hand. When the news came in of a plane hitting the Pentagon in Washington, DC, and another going down in Pennsylvania, we realized that this was an attack against America—against Americans. My heart began to race.

For a long time, none of us said a word. Disbelieving silence engulfed us like the smoke cloud that now hung over lower Manhattan. We could only stare as the horrific images rolled again and again. Reporters and newscasters speculated on possible explanations, trying to claw fragments of sense from the confusion even as survivors were being clawed out of the rubble. In our little huddled group, we all were thinking the same thing. This was no accident. It had to be a Muslim extremist attack. Nothing else made sense.

We were all very quiet the rest of the day. No one wanted to state the obvious, to say it out loud. But we could see it on our parents' faces. This had really thrown them for a loop. The risks we'd be walking into—not to mention flying into—in less than a year had suddenly hit home, all too literally. It magnified everything. Certainly the dangers, yes.

But now our friends and family saw the Muslims we were to minister to through a different lens.

We had worked so hard to raise enough financial support to be able to go to North Africa, but our previously supportive friends started coming to us with deeper concerns. "I'm sorry, but I have to withdraw our support," one friend told us. "We can't support any efforts to help those terrorists. They don't deserve to be helped." We tried to assure him that not all Muslims were terrorists. But he wouldn't hear it. Many Americans associated the Muslim world as a whole with the events of 9/11.

Like all of our fellow Americans, we were deeply wounded by the acts of terrorism that dreadful day. We were raised to be proud to be American and to never take for granted the cost that so many American men and women have paid for our freedom. We were taught to be loyal. Our allegiance was pledged. And as we prayed through our own struggles and tried to resist the discouragement we were getting from friends and family, it became clear to us that the real struggle lay in the idea that to minister to Muslims was to be disloyal to our beloved America. As we desperately tried to reconcile this in our own minds, we sought God's wisdom on the matter.

We were reminded of the Zealots in the Bible. With a singular focus of preserving their country, their religion, their language, and their way of life, they resisted and violently opposed the Romans who were occupying their land. And just like the Zealots, we can be tempted to feel that Muslims are imposing on our freedoms, our language, and our way of life in America. However, Christ wasn't intimidated by the Romans. Rather he came to love, save, and redeem them. He taught his followers to "love your enemies" and "bless those who curse you" (Matthew 5:44, NKJV). What a contrast to what the Zealots wanted to do. Their enemy was Rome. Our enemy had become al-Qaeda—and in our present day, the Islamic State. The question for us after 9/11, and still today, is, do Christ's teachings still apply to us? What if we do choose to love our enemy? What if we decide to take Jesus' words seriously and fight fire with love?

We couldn't blame our suddenly unsupportive friends for their sentiments. Even we ourselves were tempted to feel this way. I prayed for confirmation that we were indeed doing the right thing by moving to an extreme Muslim country. No one would judge us for changing our plans, shifting our focus to another part of the world. It was rational to do so, completely justifiable. But we had a conviction that came from a much higher source than the news or concerned friends and family. I wondered if this was in small part how Jesus felt as Satan tempted him in the desert. We prayed, we recalculated the cost, and we chose to stick to the last instruction given by our heavenly commander and advance as planned. We decided to keep our focus on God and the need for God's light in the dark places. Some may have wondered at the sanity of our resolution, but we found our resolve stronger than ever. We'd never expected it to be a safe ride. But our knees did get a lot more floor time after that fateful day.

By the time we finished language school and made our

final preparations, the kids were getting the idea that we weren't just preparing for a vacation. We had sold our house, our second car, our furniture, and most of our belongings in a yard sale. We should have advertised it as an estate sale, I thought. We were dying to our American dream.

We maxed out our baggage allowance for the trip with ten seventy-pound suitcases and squeezed in over one hundred pounds of homeschool materials alone. My mom cried nearly the entire drive to the airport, though she was trying not to show it. My heart was heavy for her, but I didn't know how to comfort her except to pray. I prayed for all our parents. It always seems harder for the ones staying behind.

Making our acquaintance with the revamped airport security didn't make things any easier. There was no chance of our parents walking us to the departure gate, and saying good-bye at a security checkpoint just doesn't bring quite the same sense of closure. It was one of the smaller losses of the 9/11 tragedy, but a loss nonetheless.

After a series of long flights we began our descent; the African sun dipped toward the horizon, spilling an orange glow over the dunes of the Sahara. Only God knew what awaited us this time among the ever-shifting sands.

CHAPTER 3

Putting Down Roots

NONE OF US SAID much as we disembarked and hauled our load of hand luggage down the stairs. The North African oven was in finest blistering form. It was summer, and even the relative "cool" of the evening could be as warm as 105 degrees. This was the hottest, dustiest, most oppressive air I'd ever tried to draw into my lungs.

I'd made a point of wearing thick-soled shoes as I stepped onto the sizzling tarmac and headed toward the single airport terminal. I was carrying ten-month-old Piper and holding our five-year-old Ellie's hand. Nine-year-old Heidi trailed behind. Just as she was about to take her last step off the plane she clutched her Little Mermaid backpack and abruptly turned around and headed back up the stairs. Stephen, who was minding seven-year-old Joshua and carrying far more than was practical, dropped the bags he was carrying and ran up after her. After gently hugging her, he took her by the hand and led her back down the stairs, assuring her that everything was going to be okay. She didn't resist. Her countenance shifted from fear to trust as she held tightly to her daddy's strong hand.

Stephen later confided to me the thoughts going through his mind at that point. *What have we gotten ourselves into? What have we gotten our family into?*

A tall, pretty, dark-skinned Panamanian woman met us outside the airport. Anita had worked with Lucia and was the interim director of the NGO until Stephen's arrival. She drove us to the furnished apartment we'd be staying at till we could find our own place.

While Stephen helped the kids unpack, I stood in the kitchen staring at the little two-plate gas stovetop. What was I was going to cook? *How* was I going to cook? I had never made a decent rice dish in my life.

Stephen and Joshua walked to a little boutique around the corner and returned with French bread, apricot jam, powdered milk, and a tin of Nescafe, the only coffee available. I hated instant coffee, but by this point I was ready to eat it with a spoon right out of the little can. After our thirty-hour journey, the caffeine didn't keep me awake long. I hardly remembered where I was when my head hit the pillow.

But at five or six o'clock the next morning, there was no question.

"Allaaaaaaahhhh hu akbar!"

Our apartment was right beside the mosque, which had three megaphones attached to the minaret, each facing a different direction. One just happened to be pointed right at our window. It blared the call to prayer at sunrise, three times during the day, and again in the evening when we'd just gotten the kids to bed. That first morning I sat at the little breakfast table and trailed my finger through the layer of dust that had collected overnight. There were a lot of things we were going to have to get used to.

This was a country of extremes. When it came to housing in a developing city, there was no middle ground—our options were either homes with running water and electricity in the middle-class and upper-class area, or little rooms for rent in rundown buildings where the lower class and impoverished lived. We prayed about it carefully.

We soon discovered that skin color and nationality were big indicators for the local property market. Our frustrations began to build as each day turned into another fruitless search. Our budget was being depleted by the day with our pricey apartment rental. We needed to find something soon.

Lord, I don't care what the house looks like, if it can just have one tree in the yard . . .

Trees were one of the hardest things I'd had to give up in

moving away from the abundance of trees in the Blue Ridge Mountains. I wasn't inclined to make demands of God. I really had died to all those things I'd given up. But I figured, just in case the Lord felt like it, I wouldn't mind having a tree.

A day or two later we pulled up in front of a house that looked as if it had once been painted white. In front of it, in a neat row, stood four big . . . well . . . stumps. They were trees all right, but they'd been trimmed right down to the trunk. I dared to imagine that one day they could turn into lush green shade-makers, but I didn't know what the chances were. We ventured through the front gate into the front yard. And there before our eyes stood an almond tree. With *leaves*. I was so overcome with excitement that I stopped and proclaimed on the spot, "We'll take it!"

We couldn't believe our ears when the agent told us the price—it was well under our target! At last, we had a house. Over the months we managed to accumulate enough paraphernalia to make the inside feel like home. And that yard? Apart from our almond tree, I hadn't expected much in the way of greenery. But in just a few months, to our astonishment, we were practically living in a jungle! Everything in the garden had been trimmed down to the root when we'd first come. Now several hibiscus bushes had bloomed, and a small mango tree bore fruit. The four stumps in front turned out to be Neem trees and grew into wonderful shade-givers. God had not only answered my insignificant request but had also poured out this blessing in great abundance. As we admired our incredible oasis in the desert, we thought back to the word in Isaiah 41:18-20 that God had given us in preparation for our coming:

> I will make rivers flow on barren heights,
>   and springs within the valleys.
> I will turn the desert into pools of water,
>   and the parched ground into springs.
> I will put in the desert
>   the cedar and the acacia, the myrtle and the olive.
> I will set junipers in the wasteland,
>   the fir and the cypress together,
> so that people may see and know,
>   may consider and understand,
> that the hand of the LORD has done this,
>   that the Holy One of Israel has created it.

As our garden flourished, so did our faith, though it would inevitably be challenged beyond what we could imagine.

The daily call to prayer was an effective alarm clock every morning and evening. The mosques were everywhere. From our house, you could turn almost any direction and see one within walking distance. On Fridays the prayer call would ring out from the loudspeakers multiple times throughout the day, and the afternoon was filled with preaching or reciting of the Qur'an.

Although it took some getting used to, eventually we

found the call to prayer inspiring. They were saying some beautiful things like "God is the greatest," "I bear witness that there is none worthy of worship except God," and "prayer is better than sleep." We could learn a thing or two from their devotion to prayer, even if there was an element of religiosity to it. Most of them sincerely wanted to serve and worship God. We prayed for them during their call to prayer, aching for them to know that God didn't demand performance, but that he had made a way to have a personal relationship through his Son. But how were we going to share this profound and liberating truth with a people so content with and proud of their religious culture?

CHAPTER 4

Finding Our Way

"**WELCOME!** Come in out of the cold!"

It was eighty degrees, but that was winter in this country. The old woman at the lancet arch doorway of the terra-cotta house was waving her arms and smiling broadly as we walked up.

We had just finished a five-hour drive into the interior of the desert, a much-anticipated trek to a small village. The woman welcoming us warmly was the mother of Ali, a new dear friend.

Stephen had met Ali, a cheerful Arab in his early twenties, while continuing his French studies at the Alliance Française. He enjoyed Ali's intelligence and thoughtful perspective, and the two of them would spend hours in conversation. Ali was a good practicing Muslim, and Stephen was attracted to his positive, kind, compassionate nature. He described Ali as "a man of peace."

As their friendship grew, Stephen had had the opportunity to talk to Ali about Jesus. Though he was receptive, Ali came from a very proud religious family connected to one of the most important imams in the country. Confessing faith in Jesus would likely have resulted in total rejection by his family, and in this culture, family ties ran deeper than desert wells. You married in your tribe, stayed with your tribe, and took care of your parents when they were old. To lose family was to lose everything. So Stephen simply invested in that friendship, prayed for Ali daily, and began discipling him like a son.

"I wonder if he does actually believe," Stephen told me once. "But he just can't say that out loud because of his family." Stephen wondered this because Ali was constantly sharing with his friends and family the things that Stephen was teaching him—which were primarily the teachings of Jesus. "You know, if someone strikes you on the cheek, you should turn the other cheek," Ali would tell one of his brothers.

We grew to love our frequent trips to see Ali's family. Being received into the family's well-kept, spacious home was always a treat. Wooden doors led into the *salon*, a large carpeted living room lined with *matelas*, foam mattresses covered with beautiful fabric, used for visiting during the day and sleeping on at night. Every time we'd arrive, our hosts would welcome us with *shish kabobs*. The char-grilled camel kabobs consisted of heart, stomach, liver, and even the camel hump! Though the taste was good, the texture was another story. But after our nearly daylong drive across the face of the moon, with only dry snacks and rationed water to keep us going, *shish kabobs* were always a welcome appetizer.

It was with Ali's family that we learned an unspoken cultural rule: Never finish your food. Of course this is the opposite of Western society, where we're taught to show gratitude by eating all of our food. "Think of all the starving children in Africa," we're told. But if we did this where we lived *in* Africa, the children would actually starve. They were allowed to eat only once the adults had had their fill. If we finished everything on our plates, the host assumed she (or they) had not provided sufficiently. This was a source of great shame, and the family would keep the food coming regardless of how poor they might be. In our initial ignorance, trying to be polite and grateful as they brought us plate after plate of food, we would stuff ourselves almost to the point of throwing up. But at last we learned the art of convincing them over a plate of leftovers that we were in fact well stuffed. A loud burp was the most effective and polite way to end the argument!

As guests in their home, we were expected to do nothing but lie around, chat, eat, and sleep. Droves of extended relatives and friends from far and wide would come to visit with us; with people in and out of the house from dawn till dusk, we were never quite able to figure out exactly who was who.

The kids enjoyed playing with the younger relatives and taking advantage of the satellite TV. I loved hanging out with Ali's mother and grandmother.

I was given a local name, *Mariam*, which I shared with one of Ali's sisters. Stephen was also honored with his own local name, *Cheikh-Brahim*, after the well-known imam of the tribe. Stephen earned the respect of the men during their long evenings of discussions out in the courtyard. Our kids were thrilled as they were given several local names to choose from. We'd found our adoptive family, and we felt very much at home.

On later trips to their village we started a tradition of taking a goat with us as a gift. Mister Goat would always ride in style, strapped to the roof racks of our land cruiser in a rice sack, with nothing but his little head sticking out. At least he had a scenic view.

One particular goat-laden journey started with a flat tire a couple hundred kilometers outside the city. Stephen managed to get it fixed, and in half an hour we were on our way again. A little while later, there was a startled cry from the back seat. "Eughh! What's that?"

I turned to have a look. A suspicious yellow liquid was trickling down the back windows. We all knew exactly what it was. Apparently there was a leak in the goat bag.

"We should have taken him off for a pit stop when we changed the tire," Joshua offered.

"Ew, gross! It *stinks*!" Ellie moaned. "I think it's leaking in the car!"

"We'd better pull over, Stephen," I said with a laugh. We pulled up on the roadside and all piled out for the second time to investigate the problem.

"*Bleeeeeehhh!*" the poor goat cried in disdain. Stephen removed the goat to inspect the damage and discovered that a suitcase had been unceremoniously christened.

When we finally reached the house, the relieved culprit was removed from his throne and led away. When we came back outside a few minutes later, he'd paid the ultimate penalty and was hanging from a tree. The carcass would hang, unrefrigerated, as it was stripped down over the next two or three days, depending on how many guests there were. The head, a delicacy, was always saved for last or for the guests of honor.

On day three of our visit we went on a little outing to an oasis a couple of hours away. On the way we stopped for tea at a neat little spot between some towering dunes. We could even see mountains in the distance that reminded us of New Mexico. Ali had come prepared with mint tea, a pot, and some charcoal. We set up our little picnic as the kids took off to go and play. In a few minutes they were no more than tiny dots on the dunes. Because I was the only woman—and this was a cultural tradition—I started making the tea.

We sat for a while enjoying the pleasant company and our teatime in the desert, and then Ali brought out his cooking pot and started trying to heat up whatever was inside. He didn't seem to be having much success. After a while he gave up and told us to call the kids to come and eat. He placed the offering down in front of us. There, staring back at us from atop his silver platter, with eyeballs still intact and tongue hanging out, sat our goat's head.

By this point in our North African experience, we'd eaten goat head a few times, but it had always been dressed up with plenty of French fries or couscous around it. Not this time. The head was simply plopped on the platter with a little juice around and nothing but a baguette for dipping with. Ali found a rock and completed the "final touches" of his food preparation with a *thud* to give us access to the goat brains.

How were my kids going to react to . . . well, not exactly your average afternoon picnic? To my relief, they just glanced at the plate and sat down without a word. The baguette was passed around for everyone to break off a piece, then we all dug in. As usual, Stephen had no qualms. He even had some of the tongue and an eyeball, which was a local favorite. Whenever we'd had goat head before, the youngest boy in the family we were visiting would always want the eyeball, but because we were the guests, the dad wouldn't let him have it. Naturally, I would always plead the kid's case: "Aw, no it's fine, *really* . . . give him the eyeball."

The culture took a lot of getting used to. For example, we quickly realized that appearances played a big role in this culture, but in a very different way than they did in the United States. The women felt sorry for me because of my slim wrist and ankle bones. Wrists and ankles were the only body parts to be shown off from under clothing, so fat and juicy was the only way to go. One lady gave me a pitying look when she noticed my slightly protruding collarbone. "I'm so sorry," she said, the way someone might comfort a sick person.

The women were enamored of beautiful things and loved to dress up, even just to go into town. They could be among the poorest, but they'd still have on their "good hijabs" to look nice in public. And they would decorate their hands and feet with henna on most special occasions, such as weddings and holidays.

Weddings were an elaborate cultural experience, to say the least. The event, which took place over three days, always involved lots of food and people. In most cases the wedding was really an exchange between the two sets of parents, who had arranged the marriage. The groom and bride wouldn't even be together when they were officially married. The groom would go to the mosque while the bride's female entourage spent the entire first day doing her up with braids, beads, make-up, and henna all over her arms, hands, ankles, and feet. She would finally show up at the wedding at about midnight, completely covered in black from head to toe, with no more than a slit for her eyes. The groom and all of the women would then go into one of the rooms for a viewing of the human art piece. This was often the bride's favorite part—she got to show off her beautiful henna and get her picture taken for friends and family. The bride would remain completely covered during the second day of the wedding, and on the third she could reveal her face once again.

Our girls loved these weddings, particularly the music and dancing. Even at six years old, our sweet quiet little Ellie loved dancing in the middle of a circle of women as they cheered her on. Little did I know it then, but this experience birthed a lifelong passion in Ellie for dance.

In the beginning our broken French got us around with making friends, doing basic chores, and shopping at the markets. But we soon realized that the bit of French we knew was not going to suffice for intimate friendships. Stephen had been improving on his French at the Alliance Française, but he realized we needed to do more than that. French was taught in the schools, but the majority of the poor were illiterate, and even those who went to school didn't learn enough French to master the language. So we invested ourselves in learning the Arabic dialect because most of the other ethnic groups also knew at least some.

Stephen was particularly gifted at it. The locals were always amazed at this white man who would come and sit on the floor in their house, telling them stories in their language and rounding them off with a good moral or proverb. His newly acquired language skills also came in very handy at the frequent police checks we'd encounter when traveling out of the city. The police would take any opportunity to try to get a bribe from a white man, but Stephen would always catch them off-guard with his charm and quick wit. One local proverb he used that always seemed to break the ice was, "When a bird enters a forest, he must sing like the birds of that forest (for survival)." We'd usually pull away from a group of laughing uniformed men.

Learning the language was only the beginning of understanding this country. The country's complex cultural and ethnic structure and history would take many years to fully comprehend. The population, which numbered just over three million, was made up of three main people groups and several smaller tribes. Navigating the myriad of tribes, castes, classes, and systems of nobility was like trying to follow a very tangled ball of string that stretched way back into the country's ethnic, social, and geographical history. Slavery had only been abolished in the early 1980s, and the psychological and spiritual effects would take a long time to filter out of the culture. Actual slavery was still practiced in many parts of the country.

Class disparity played a large role in the living conditions. In some neighborhoods the black ethnic group still worked for the Arabs, and even though they were supposedly "freed" slaves, they were paid very little, if they were paid at all. In some of the Arabs' minds, their darker-skinned neighbors were still there to serve them. We were thankful for the many wonderful Arabs whose broader worldview had come a long way from racism.

As we first began to navigate this complex social structure, Stephen and I found we had an unfair advantage. Simply being white and American, which apparently automatically classified us as "rich," earned us most people's respect by default. A lot of them seemed quite proud to be a friend of an American. But not all. Some in the upper class grew cooler around us when they realized we associated with the poorest of the poor as well. They seemed a little bothered that we gave equal friendship to people in the worst areas of town, sitting in the dirt and eating from the same bowl as our "low-class" friends. Was this how Jesus felt, getting abuse from the religious leaders for eating with the prostitutes and tax collectors?

CHAPTER 5

The American Dilemma

"SHE'S FROM AMERICA, and she's married to the same husband, the father of all her children. He doesn't even drink! And"—my neighbor, unaware that I could understand her Arab dialect, switched to a gossipy whisper—"they even pray and fast!" There were clucks of amazement around the room, and a few pairs of eyes threw astonished glances my way.

She had invited me over to break fast with her. The month of Ramadan, the most important on the Islamic calendar, entailed daily fasting from sunup till sundown. Ramadan literally means "scorched," which was very befitting—people were not even allowed to swallow their own spit during the day. Most seemed to love expressing their righteous suffering.

During Ramadan we'd often be invited to break fast with friends, and in that case I'd fast intentionally that day and express to them that I was praying for them and their country during my recent fasting. This was met with great appreciation. The fact that Christians fasted at all was a secret that people in their country hadn't heard before, and they were intrigued. "Are you fasting today?" was the inevitable question many would ask us throughout the day.

"Well, as a follower of Christ I do fast," I would reply, "but I won't tell you if I'm fasting today because that's something between me and God." They were completely astonished.

We had realized that the labels "American" and "Christian" were practically interchangeable to the people we met— which, by virtue of Western media, meant that "Hollywood" and "Christian" were also interchangeable. And this was problematic. Their only window into Christianity, unfortunately, was what they saw on TV, and needless to say, Britney Spears and reruns of *Dallas* hadn't exactly painted a moral picture.

So we needed some new labels. We decided to stop saying, "I'm a Christian" and would say instead, "I'm a follower of Christ." In the local language, this literally translated as "I'm a student of Jesus." We avoided saying we were American when we could—to a large degree, it made sense for us to drop our American identity. This wasn't easy. We were proud to be American, but holding our American citizenship in equal value to our heavenly citizenship would have limited our witness. God is not American, and he doesn't advance his kingdom on earth through our Christian American means.

In order to reach these people, we needed to contextualize, to learn to appreciate their God-given culture, food, and traditions, to become *like them*, to see them through God's eyes. As we fell in love with our new country, especially its people, we understood in a new way why Jesus gave up his Godly form, came down to us in the flesh to meet us on our level, and called us to imitate his example. Fasting with our friends during Ramadan was a simple yet powerful way to do that.

Prayer was another easy way of breaking down misconceptions. Whenever we'd visit people, if they had any issues they were dealing with, we'd immediately drop everything and ask whether we could pray for them in the name of Jesus. They never refused us and were always thankful.

We found it quite a challenge to do our work projects during Ramadan. Most of the students just didn't show up, either physically or mentally. Often we'd just have to cancel classes. But the nights were a great time for visiting—people were in such high spirits after the daily fast ended (and ironically, more food was sold and consumed during Ramadan than at any other time of year). We found the late nights a bit of a challenge, but it was nothing that a cup of coffee in the morning wouldn't solve. I'm not sure where Stephen found his boost of energy every morning. It was clearly a God thing. So many times during visits with friends I would sit across the room just watching how Stephen effortlessly showed the love of Christ to these wonderful people, his face aglow as he smiled and conversed with them. They were clearly aware that this "man of God," as the locals often referred to him, loved them dearly.

Other things within the culture were harder to get used to, though. The rules of public affection, for instance, were totally foreign to our Western minds. Not even being able to hold Stephen's hand when we walked together drove me a little crazy at first. Stephen and I felt compelled to make a point of expressing our love for each other in public as much as we could without being too physical. We hoped to show a good example of a Christlike marriage in this divorce-torn society, so we compensated for the lack of physical affection by being extra affectionate verbally and smiling at each other a lot. That was our normal behavior, so it didn't take much extra effort. But it certainly seemed to strike other people as interesting and different.

We'd realized that if we were going to settle in here and not go crazy in the face of everything that was so different, we needed to maintain a good attitude. The people of this impoverished nation seldom complained. They didn't have Walmart and online shopping and twenty fast-food menus to choose from—they ate rice and couscous every day of the week. But they never moaned about it. That humbled us. We'd been spoiled back home. The kids would complain sometimes, as kids do, but Stephen and I tried not to nurture it, least of all contribute to it. Attitudes are contagious, and it worked both ways. If we could learn to love the country and cultivate positivity, the kids would catch on.

CHAPTER 6

Not Forgotten

"THE COUNTRY GOD HAS FORGOTTEN." We'd come across the phrase before making the move to our new home in North Africa. Even Lonely Planet had struggled to find anything positive to say about this place. Everyone focused on all the negatives, and it was easy to reach that conclusion with a tourist mind-set. We'd been guilty of the same negativity on outreach. But when we started to see the country through God's eyes, we could appreciate its beauty. And as we were beginning to see from our relationships, God had certainly not forgotten this place.

Back home we were considered "missionaries," but we now lived and worked in a country whose borders were closed to

Christianity, though thankfully not to Christians. It was not against the law for us to be Christians, but it was illegal for locals to convert to anything other than Islam. We wanted to be identified in all honesty and integrity with exactly what we were actually doing with our NGO—relief and development. However, we were committed to staying true to our most important identity as followers of Christ, ready in and out of season to share the love of God with anyone.

We didn't consider ourselves to be "undercover missionaries." We would live our faith out loud through our actions without overuse of words that were offensive in our new home. Our ministry would be all about building bridges of trust and relationship through the practice of servanthood. We trusted that Stephen's post as NGO director would open the doors to start serving our new host country effectively. As we'd seen during our first visit, there was overwhelming physical need in this country, and we'd been given the opportunity to help improve the quality of life.

So if we were here to set the captives free, what better place to start than in the prisons? Stephen began to teach English classes in the men's prison, and the authorities were very open to the idea of nutrition, hygiene, and literacy classes in the boys' prison.

The men's prison held around nine hundred men in a drab, concrete building built for six hundred. When Stephen first stepped through the front gate, he was overwhelmed by unpleasant smells. The dilapidated building and poor plumbing could not accommodate the number of prisoners and guards. The place was swarming with flies and other vermin. There was clearly a shortage of water and basic needs, and there were no beds—only several small, unventilated rooms where the men slept in whatever tiny spot they could find.

Stephen decided that English classes would give him access to the prisoners until he could assess what needs our organization could meet. The room provided for the class was far too small for the number of interested inmates. Many of the men were obviously hardened criminals, but some of them just happened to have been in the wrong place at the wrong time and were serving far too much time for a crime they hadn't committed. Stephen struck up a friendship with one man who picked up the English almost effortlessly. Kind, intelligent, and dignified, he seemed totally out of place. Stephen learned that the young man's father had been convicted of a crime years earlier and was serving a life sentence. The man had become old and frail, and after many failed attempts to get him released, the young man offered to finish out his father's sentence instead.

The main work of our NGO was still the project at the women's prison, which involved taking hygiene products and food to the women and teaching some basic nutrition and healthcare classes. A humble and pure-hearted local Christian named Fatu ran the sewing classes, and I offered to join her and help facilitate. Any help I could offer seemed like such a tiny drop in the vast and parched desert of needs in this country.

The women's prison had moved to a different building—smaller, but better kept. The women were very enthusiastic about the sewing classes, though I didn't feel much better equipped as a sewing teacher than I had during our short-term ministry—but at least now we could understand each other a little more. Despite the better conditions, roaches still scattered every time I sat down on the floor and began taking out the needles and thread. There was very little room on the floor in the small room, and I found myself fighting claustrophobia. Often the women were so excited to see me, jostling to get a seat close to me, it felt as if they were going to sit in my lap. One of the ladies—one of the many named Fatima—weighed in at more than four hundred pounds and was one of the kindest and most jovial women I had ever met. She also had a tremendous sense of humor and constantly had the room roaring in laughter.

Each time Fatu and I arrived for sewing class, the atmosphere of the room lightened. It was as if we brought sunshine to their vitamin D–deficient lives. I wasn't sure what God could do through my teaching them basic sewing skills, but I had to constantly remind myself to trust him to be working on a larger pattern and tying the threads behind the scenes.

During our time preparing for our work here, Stephen had learned about the idea of microcredit initiatives, which involved small loans of anything from fifty to five hundred dollars being granted to promising entrepreneurs in disadvantaged environments, to be paid back within a reasonable timeframe once the business was up and running. The concept had been implemented to great success in other developing nations. To a Western mind-set and wallet, the loans seemed relatively insignificant and easy to fund. But the money and motivation attached to each loan certainly went a long way in the third-world environment, empowering many families to become self-sustaining.

Stephen decided to give the concept a test run with an ex-prisoner who wanted to open a small shop at the main fishing harbor. At first it seemed to be going well, and the man repaid a portion of the loan. But soon the payments began to taper off. Though he was committed to making his business work, this man wasn't all committed to paying back the loan. We soon realized that in this country and culture, a loan to a friend is seen as a gift. The traditional microloan structure simply wouldn't work here. So Stephen began working on a new strategy. We would fund cooperatives instead of a single person for the purpose of accountability. And there must be women involved in every one.

The women we encountered generally seemed to be more responsible to their families and serious about putting the money where it needed to go. They also seemed a bit more convinced that the right thing to do would be to repay the loan so that we could fund other women who also desperately needed to provide for their children. The first cooperative was established with five women who wanted to open a boutique.

The co-op consisted of the mother of an ex-prisoner from the juvenile prison, two of her sisters, and two friends. Each of the women except for one was divorced and had several children to support on her own—an all-too-common scenario, we found. They all were living well below the poverty line and weren't able to send their malnourished children to school. They purchased wood that came from recycled shipping pallets and constructed a small shack with a door and a window through which to sell their goods. Besides special items like Coca-Cola and candy, they primarily sold basic staples such as rice, sugar, and flour: things that local women needed to buy each day for preparing meals. The women were enthusiastic and committed to the business, and they had soon grown it enough to pay off their loan. They added a small carry-out restaurant to their successful boutique, and each time we stopped by to see how things were going, we would buy a sandwich or some things that we needed from the boutique. It was gratifying to see the children transition from hungry, unenergetic stick figures to normal, fun-loving, healthier children being reprimanded for not sitting still during our visit. The women were happier, and soon all of their children were going to school. We started funding more cooperatives with a minimum of five women or sometimes a family. Some ran boutiques that sold basic foods. Some would sell clothes products, too—beautifully dyed hijabs on one side, food goods on the other side. These women were incredibly resourceful and motivated.

Soon the initiative had expanded all over the city, and

though it wasn't one hundred percent successful, we were encouraged to see the fruits abounding. Families were climbing out of poverty and given a chance to thrive. It was really benefiting single moms in particular; they could now support themselves, and some were able to send their kids to school for the first time.

I was particularly inspired by Zeinab. Zeinab was forced to marry her first husband, who was much older than she, when she was only thirteen. Two children later, her husband divorced her, leaving her and the children with no provision. She went back to her family, but they didn't have the means to care for Zeinab and the children either, so she was encouraged to find another husband to provide. Two or three more husbands and several more children later, Zeinab found herself desperate to provide the most basic needs of her children, so she turned to prostitution, a crime that landed her in prison. I was struck by Zeinab's beauty and intelligence when I first met her in the prison sewing class. She loved sewing and excelled in everything she was given to do. When Zeinab was released from prison, we gave her a sewing machine and a small microcredit loan. We loved being able to help in a practical way that allowed people to maintain their dignity while developing their God-given abilities.

As the work expanded, we realized that serving people on a practical level meant that we could reach them on a relational and spiritual level. Visiting the business cooperatives on a regular basis gave us great opportunities to build relationships. Often Stephen would just sit for hours with the women and their families who ran the businesses, telling stories from the Bible that demonstrated good business practice and wise decision making. Muslims have a deep respect for Jesus, whom they believe to be only a prophet. And because theirs is such an oral culture, they love stories. We began to incorporate stories into our sewing classes, aiming for ones that instilled character. We'd get into discussions about honesty, humility, and even marriage. We were thrilled that God had given us this natural, effective, nonthreatening tool to teach our friends about Jesus.

"I would like to extend an invitation to the good men of this church to join me in reaching out to the men of the prison here in the city. I need a man who will love some of the most desperate men I've ever seen. The need is great, but the opportunity for God's love and grace to abound to the prisoners is even greater. I would like to challenge us with the words of Jesus Christ in Matthew 25:36: 'I was in prison and you came to me.' I have seen Jesus in the prison here. Will you come to him?"

Stephen made this appeal one Friday after the expat church service. As the prison work expanded and other projects were launched, Stephen began to fully understand his limited human capacity and the need for more help. He asked the "Lord of the harvest" to send workers and sensed God prompting him to tap into a very underused resource: the expat Protestant church. No locals were allowed to attend because of an agreement between the government and the Catholic church we rented a room from, so our church consisted mostly of black Africans from other countries. Many of these believers had moved to our host city to look for a way to make a living. And in that treasure box, Stephen found one of our most valuable gems: a gentle-natured Congolese man named Timothy.

As Timothy listened to Stephen's appeal, his heart began to burn. He decided immediately that he would volunteer. But by the time he got to Stephen, several men were already talking to him. Timothy assumed he was too late and so went home. But he couldn't get the idea of working in the prisons out of his head.

The following week he visited some friends in the country to the south. While Timothy was at a church service there, the pastor stopped right in the middle of his sermon and said, "I believe we need to stop right now and pray. I believe that there is someone here tonight who needs to ask God for something, and I believe God wants to give you the desire of your heart." Timothy felt as if the pastor were staring right at him. Before he realized that the words were coming out of his mouth, Timothy prayed, "God, I want to work for you in the prisons."

Timothy had moved to the country as a refugee just a couple of years before. An intelligent and educated man, he had found a job teaching and used his income to buy a vehicle that he used as a taxi on the side. The first passenger Timothy picked up after returning from visiting his friends was a big, bearded man with long ungroomed hair. Timothy hesitated but then stopped to let him. After the normal series of greetings, Timothy asked, "Where to, sir?"

The man looked at Timothy with a disoriented look in his dark-ringed eyes. "I just got out of prison."

"Oh?" Timothy thought back to his prayer.

As they started chatting, the man told Timothy he'd been in prison for shooting an American and had just been released. We would later find out that this was the man who had shot the American and his daughter in their car at the beach. The family had come to talk to their assailant in prison about what he'd done and had offered forgiveness. They had also brought him food and clothing. This had so impacted the man that he now wanted to find a way to help others in prison.

Timothy's heart began to beat rapidly. God was working in this moment, he could tell. "I know of a man who works in the prisons!" Timothy told his passenger excitedly. "I can introduce you!"

Stephen was thrilled when Timothy got in touch, and they arranged to meet the next day.

"I can't get over the fact that the man I shot was willing to forgive me," exclaimed the ex-prisoner. "His offer of forgiveness has changed my life! Now I just want to help other people."

As they began discussing what the man had done and his desire to change and reconcile his wrongdoing by "giving back," Stephen looked at Timothy. "What do you think we can do to help this man, Timothy?"

Without hesitation, Timothy laid out a thoughtful plan for how the man could prove to society that he was indeed changed. Stephen just sat and listened, stunned by Timothy's wisdom.

From that meeting an unbreakable and God-ordained bond of brotherhood was forged between Stephen and Timothy. Stephen immediately saw something in him, and when he asked Timothy to teach at the boy's prison, Timothy was overjoyed. He felt that his calling was confirmed.

A couple of days later, Stephen took Timothy to the boys' prison to introduce him to the prison director and prison guards. All the employees at the boys' prison warned Timothy upfront, "There's no way you'll be able to teach these boys. We've tried. They're unteachable. It's impossible to even get them to come to class."

Timothy—soft-spoken, five-foot-seven, and one of the kindest Africans we had ever met—looked at Stephen with intense concern on his face. "I think this might be a bad idea," he said. "I'm not sure I can handle those boys."

Stephen smiled at him. "Timothy, you are a teacher, right? Go. Go and do what God put in your heart to do. Don't listen to the others. You can do it."

So Timothy persevered and kept praying. In just a few weeks, Timothy could walk up to the boys wherever they were and say, "Come to class," and all of them would follow him until the room was packed. After a while the mullah asked Timothy for help getting the boys rounded up for his Qur'anic class!

It was settled. Timothy left his previous job teaching and his taxi business and became Stephen's main man in the project work.

✠

We had started sewing classes outside the prisons because the project Fatu and I had been conducting at the prison for the last year was bursting at the seams. Even women who had been released were returning with their bits of material and begging to be let back in! The class had grown so big that the guards stopped allowing the released women reentry on sewing-class days.

The women were so excited to be making things they could actually sell in order to provide for their families. One of the released woman—unfortunately nicknamed Tutu-bad-teeth for reasons you can probably guess—told me she was saving up for something. Then one day she disappeared. When she finally showed up again a few weeks later, she brought a big smile with her. She'd bought some dentures. Her nickname was Tutu-good-teeth from then on!

But we knew it wasn't just the money that kept them coming back. It was the fellowship. They simply loved to be heard, even if we couldn't always understand everything in the conversation. They just appreciated that we were there. This new sense of value was not something they wanted to give up just because they weren't behind bars anymore.

When we decided to start hosting classes outside the prison, Fatu and I talked about wanting to create a sustainable project that would continue beyond us. After much prayer, we felt we should propose that one of the ex-prisoners host the gathering. At first, this idea seemed ridiculous to me. These women were very poor and lived in small rented rooms with little to no electricity. Not really expecting much of a response, I put the word out. To my surprise and delight, the women started fighting over who would have the honor to be the hostess!

Although moving to the women's homes had been an improvement from the prison, the interest in the classes had kept growing until once again chaos reigned. I was thankful when Phoebe, a young friend of ours from the States, joined us in North Africa to help with the work. When Phoebe arrived at her first class, twenty women were crowded around me on the floor, all wanting to show me their work, asking for more thread, another needle, ten of them needing help at the same time . . . it was enough to give anyone a headache. "Sewing teacher" wouldn't have been Phoebe's first choice of occupation, just as it wasn't mine. But her strength was in the creative side—she was great at coming up with new ideas and designs for wall hangings, bookmarks, and other little things the women could make.

Phoebe also joined me in the prison work as we continued to visit the women and teach sewing and health classes. While she couldn't indulge her evangelistic gift as much as she would have liked, her smiling cheerfulness hugely impacted every person she came in contact with. As Stephen often pointed out, a single light bulb in the lighting aisle at the hardware store makes very little impact, but the same bulb lit in a place of utter darkness makes a huge impact.

Someone around the sewing circle sneezed.

"God bless you," a girl named Mouna said, glancing up.

A hush settled over the room. Then another woman lashed out. "Why did you not say the traditional words? Are you a *Christian* now?"

Mouna had shown a lot more interest in the Bible stories we shared in class than the others had. Phoebe, Fatu, and I held our breath, waiting to hear her answer. To our surprise, she replied, "So what if I am?"

Mouna was clearly interested in the gospel and probed Phoebe with a lot of questions. "Why does Fatu tell me I need to forgive the other women who are mean to me when I haven't done anything to them?" she asked. We prayed that God would keep drawing her in.

It was an exciting day when we showed the women *The JESUS Film.* The film had become one of our greatest resources, not to mention a great asset for our language learning. We'd prayed there would be no distractions or negative reactions as we showed the film. And thankfully, all of the women seemed to enjoy it. At the scene where John the Baptist comes out and tells the people asking to be saved that they should sell their possessions and give the money to the poor, the women got excited and started nudging each other, remarking, "*Skeet! Skeet!*" (The equivalent of "That's awesome!")

When the film was over we all sat in a circle on the floor and asked the women to share something they'd learned or liked about sewing class. When it came to Fatu's turn, she looked around the circle for a moment. Fatu was such a cherished coworker in this place. She was one of few who were bold in sharing their faith, and she was coming under much persecution for it. Though married to a man who was supposedly a believer, Fatu started showing up at work with black eyes and bald spots. He'd begun beating her when she couldn't produce a son, then beat her more when she refused to let his second wife join them in their home. Even in the midst of this, she was such a woman of grace.

So imagine my shock at the words that came out of her mouth now.

"I am not perfect," she said gently. "And I have made mistakes. I wish to apologize to each of you for an offense I may have caused."

These words? From Fatu? The kindest, most humble, most honorable woman who'd ever been a part of these classes? I was appalled that she felt like she had anything to apologize to these women for. Many of them owed *her* an apology, I thought—they had said hateful things to or about Fatu and had been cruel at times because of her decision to follow Christ.

But I sensed God telling me to stay quiet. He knew exactly what he was up to.

The effect of her words was immediate and powerful. One by one, the other women started covering their faces with their hijabs, hiding their crying. As we went around the rest of the circle, the spirit of repentance and forgiveness caught like wildfire. Each person, even those who had been the most spiteful, apologized for her behavior toward the others. By the time it was Mouna's turn, all she could do was sob. A short time later she professed her faith in Jesus.

As we saw individual fruit through Mouna's life, we also saw amazing fruit in the class as a whole. Soon the sewing class had doubled again. We were running two classes a week with about thirty students. Most of them were faced with the task of being the sole providers for their families, but their needs went far deeper than the physical. We didn't want to turn any away, but Phoebe and I were being spread too thin. We prayed and decided to ask five of our most advanced sewers to consider volunteering as teachers. They accepted with delight. Over the next few weeks and months, they flourished in their new roles. We were overwhelmed. Faced with so much opportunity for growth and progress, Stephen and Phoebe and I began to dream: "Wouldn't it be wonderful to have a center for training up more teachers who could run with the vision themselves? Not just in the sewing class but also in other vocational skills?"

CHAPTER 7

Culture Shock

"MOMMY! WHY IS THE SKY DRIPPING?" Piper was mesmerized. It was the first real rain we'd seen in two years—and the first rain she could remember. As we taxied to the gate after our long flight, plastering ourselves to the windows and watching the rain in awe, we were in high spirits.

We'd come back to visit friends, family, and supporters in the United States for the first time since we'd left for our North African country. It was strange, feeling cool air as we stepped onto the breezeway and being greeted by security guards who spoke English. We'd heard the term "reverse culture shock" but hadn't expected it to be this tangible. As we tried to hurry our way through JFK to catch our connecting flight, the kids kept getting distracted by the water fountains. Every few minutes they were suddenly "thirsty" and would run back to the fountain to have a drink. They couldn't get over the fact that they could get cold water at just the press of a little lever.

We had been told that two years was a good period to stay put in a new country before returning home for furlough. A taste of home too soon, in the midst of the hard adjustment to a new country, might cause us to prematurely engage the "ejector seat." It had been sound advice. The first year had been incredibly challenging, and it had taken a full eighteen months to get through our culture shock and begin to truly feel at home. We were very glad we'd waited the full two years before our first furlough.

The interstate was the first real scare of our reverse culture shock. Not having driven in a fast vehicle on a smooth road since we'd left the States, I was a bit terrified by the speed. "Slow down for potholes! Watch out for the other drivers!" I wanted to shout. My nerves calmed a little as we rolled into the placid, green suburbs. Everything was so *clean*—it was like a dream. After we got settled in my parents' house, I stood under the hot, high-pressure shower for what felt like an hour, then collapsed into bed in the air-conditioned basement bedroom. I was completely zapped after the long trip.

The reverse culture shock was amplified the next morning as I stood in Walmart with my jaw dropping to the polished floor. All this *food*. All this *stuff*. The sheer volume and variety was mind-blowing—almost disturbing. I felt like I was seeing it all for the first time.

The wondrous overabundant food supply was matched by the spiritual abundance freely available in this part of the USA. As we drove around town, we saw a church on practically every corner. We could find a sermon or worship service at the touch of a remote or radio button. It was a gluttonous buffet. Other parts of the world hadn't even had a morsel to taste. How had I never noticed this before? It seemed that there were more churches in our little American town than there were Christians in our entire country in North Africa.

We tried to convey some of our fresh-eyed perspective to our friends, supporters, and church family. As we did the "rounds" this time, we of course had a lot more insight and passion in sharing about the needs in our field. For the most part, people seemed very responsive. Our stories moved them beyond the pages of *National Geographic*—they were latching onto the projects and wanting to participate. They committed to sending sewing supplies, investing in the microcredit projects and doing whatever else they could to help. Perhaps even more valuable was the spiritual and moral support they pledged, promising to pray for us on a daily basis. This was the beauty of raising our own support—while it did mean a lot more legwork and administration, it also raised a lot more awareness and transformed "distance donors" into real partners in the journey.

While most of the response was positive, some people were still rather resistant to supporting our work because of the many misconceptions and stereotypes that now clung ever more tenaciously to the word *Muslim*. But we had Muslim friends we worked with every day, so the idea that every Muslim was a terrorist was ludicrous. Our friend Ali was more kind hearted and gentle natured than many Americans we'd ever worked with—or even than a lot of the Christians we knew. We wished we could just take everyone with us to meet him and the other people we were sharing our lives and hearts with. We prayed that God would give our American support- ers the heart he'd given us for our Muslim friends.

Stephen pointed out that whatever religion a person had grown up in was probably what they were going to believe. All the more so in a fully Islamic country, where *prescribed* religion is synonymous with culture. Islam is the school cur- riculum, the way Muslims wear their clothes and walk down the street, the way they respond to a sneeze. Religion is sim- ply not a question of personal choice. It's an identity.

Our American friends were simply afraid. They heard our message of hope. They heard our account of how wonderful and peaceful our North African friends were, but the voice of media and of militant revenge rung louder in their ears. They were convinced that every Muslim was commissioned to "kill the infidels." We tried hard to change that mind-set.

"Most of our Muslim friends don't even believe that verse is in the Qur'an—they've never fully memorized it," I would argue. We were frustrated. It seemed that the Enemy had the perfect tactic—make Muslims believe that all Christians are adulterous, drunk, promiscuous, war-loving people who have no morals . . . and make the Christians believe that all Muslims are terrorists out to obliterate anyone who is not Muslim. And why not? This is what both groups see in media and hear preached in the mosques and churches.

Muslims are not the enemy. They are people held captive by the Enemy. Too often we as Christians are quick to shoot the hostage. But the Jesus we serve came to set the captives free, and he asks us to do the same.

Wherever Stephen spoke, he pleaded from Luke 10:2: "The harvest is plentiful but the workers are few." More money and more material resources could accomplish only so much; the biggest need was always for more people simply willing to go and be used by God in his harvest field. Though many people seemed to understand our heart and our message, there were always even more who would not quite get it. People would say to us, "I'm glad you're doing what you're doing, but I'm glad he called you to do it and not me." Or they would say, "What you're doing is really admirable, but you know, we really need to focus more on the needs here at home, because we are surrounded by *so* many needs right here in our own country." I wanted to respond, "Well, it's obvious that's why God has called you and the other 999 members of your church to stay." I wanted to ask whether they'd considered the fact that there are less than three Christian workers for every one million Muslims, or whether they knew many Americans who are trying to live on less than a dollar a day. It was a little frustrating, to say the least. And I had to constantly repent of my sarcastic attitude. We could drip our drop in the ocean, but how could we change a whole mind-set? We felt a deep conviction to avoid making people feel guilty for not sharing our passion to reach the unreached, particularly Muslims. We longed for people to understand that the ultimate fuel for our zeal was to see the Father get what he alone deserves—the praise and adoration of every tribe, tongue, nation, and people. We were burdened for the Muslim people, and we were burdened to help our Christian counterparts understand God's heart for them.

We had to keep reminding ourselves that we had been *co*-missioned with God. The Holy Spirit would play his part. We could only use what God had given us—our example and our words.

As I reflect on the tension we face as American Christians—the desire to stay comfortable and safe while following a God who calls us to anything but a comfortable and safe life—I keep going back to something Stephen would say:

> We can spend our lives chasing after the next hot
> sermon, getting our heads stuck in Bible studies,
> and completely missing the whole point. Knowledge
> of the Word is imperative, but that alone is only
> half-obedience. The Word is meant to be living and
> *active*. We are certainly called to study and hide his
> word in our hearts, but if that is as far as we go with
> it, then we are like a Dead Sea—constantly taking
> in life-giving water only to let it stagnate and die

because we have no outlet for it. *"Go ye therefore"* . . .
Why don't we take him at his word?

Where is a candle more effective—in a room
filled with light, or a room filled with darkness?
Even though there are millions of unsaved people in
this country, America has light. We have the Good
News! But in much of the rest of the world, there
are millions of people who have not heard the Word
a single time. There is much darkness. So where
should I spend my time?

CHAPTER 8

What Is My Mission?

NOW THAT I HAD experienced my true purpose, I was beginning to wonder whether the "American Dream" was all it was cracked up to be. It had taken two years of sand, sweat, and tears, but I truly felt like Africa *was* where we belonged—at least for now. We'd started building something. We had dreams and vision for the work God wanted us to do. It was exciting. And hard. But God had answered our prayers and granted all of us a peace that went beyond understanding and circumstance.

I had feared that after my kids got an updated taste of what they were "missing out on" in the US, they might not want to return. To my relief, they didn't seem to mind, though I sensed a divided desire in my older two. They were being pulled between two worlds. I prayed for grace for all of them. God had been faithful thus far. Surely he would be faithful to the end of our journey.

Part of that faithfulness came in the form of a new partner to our ministry family. We had first met Grace the previous June at a conference. She had an early-childhood-education license and ten years' teaching experience and knew that her next season would be somewhere in North Africa. We'd talked briefly about the possibility of her coming to help us homeschool our kids, but nothing was definite yet. She'd decided to come for a two-month visit to scout out the situation and pray for guidance. Grace and the kids hit it off right away. And rooming with Phoebe also seemed to help Grace immensely through the culture shock. They had a few good laughs over Grace's initial interpretation of the call to prayer. The phrase being called out sounded similar to the words for rice and fish. "Why do they keep calling out recipes?" Grace wondered aloud.

Soon Grace's initial two-month commitment turned into a year and a half. During her first six months, she came to our house most mornings to help the kids with their schoolwork. She also watched the kids for us during sewing classes. She was an incredible answer to prayer. I couldn't oversee the sewing program, maintain friendships, and do all the home-schooling, but with Grace taking some of the load, I was finally able to invest intensive time in my language studies. Trying to carry on a meaningful conversation without a good level of language ability was like trying to run a race without legs. I took up language classes three days a week at a nearby language school. It was a slow process, and for the first few months I often despaired that I was not making much progress.

But even while I struggled with the language, things on the work side seemed to be taking off more than ever. Our team had doubled. We'd gotten two more well-used vehicles for our projects. The embassy had just signed a one-year contract with our NGO to fund our juvenile rehabilitation center project, the women's prison project, and most exciting of all, the creation of a vocational training and learning center. This would be key to taking our work and ministry to a whole new level.

While all of this was happening, Phoebe and Grace started a kids club in a few of our local neighborhoods. The kids club gave them opportunity to love on the children in practical ways and to provide much-needed basic education for the poorest children who would likely never have the chance to go to school. Apart from reading and writing, they also developed a wonderful curriculum to teach the kids character lessons. Phoebe wrote contextualized stories for subjects like patience, sharing, lying, and integrity, and Grace drew the contextualized illustrations. It was ingenious.

As I struggled to understand and fill my own role in the growing work, I sensed that God had bigger ideas than what I felt fit comfortably within my capacity. The Lord kept opening more doors and helping me realize that yes, I did have a joint calling with Stephen, but that God had also placed an individual call on my life, a purpose that no man—even one as selfless and Spirit-empowered as Stephen—could ever fulfill. Stephen could not reach out to women in this conservative Muslim society. He was discipling several men but had no connection with their wives or daughters.

This was where my divinely appointed puzzle piece fit. The local women were clearly on God's heart, and I felt a deep conviction to love and serve them. I felt both liberated and exhilarated to realize that God had given me a personal part to play on this sandy stage. But the question still remained: "How can I do it all? I'm only one person, Lord." My hands were plenty full with my own family and their needs, yet God was bidding me to reach women and children with his love. I felt a certainty about both callings, but I often felt overwhelmed as I sought a balance.

I had come to this country knowing that my primary role would be to support Stephen and take care of our family and the kids' schooling. I had resolved from the beginning to be the best wife and mother I could be. But as fulfilling as that was, I couldn't escape the feeling that there was more to my calling. Before moving to Africa, I assumed I had to make a choice to be either completely wife and mom or completely "field worker." Surely God wouldn't expect me to do both.

The Enemy started working overtime in his efforts to convince me that I wasn't competent enough to do any of it well. Guilt became an unwanted guest in my heart, eating away at any self-confidence and motivation I had managed to store away. When my children made wrong decisions and had to be disciplined, I blamed myself: *If I had only been there instead of at sewing class, I could have taken care of Joshua and Ellie's argument. If I hadn't waited until the third cup of tea before leaving Aicha's house last night, dinner would have been at a decent hour and the kids wouldn't be so irritable and hungry.*

As if my own condemnation wasn't enough, I wondered whether I was being scrutinized by a couple of other American moms who were living there in the capital and happily homeschooling and taking care of their own homes while their husbands did the "outside work."

"I feel like my sole mission and calling right now is my children," they proclaimed. "I feel like God has called me as a mom to pour all of my life into them while we have them."

Of course! It made perfect sense. Was I wrong to have such a deep desire to reach out? I *did* want to pour my life into my children—to give them a perfect, sheltered life completely sterile of any outside darkness. But the reality of the need and brokenness surrounding us was unavoidable. We are all surrounded by broken people no matter where we are in the world. I felt compelled to minister with Stephen. I decided to place my deep sense of guilt and incompetence before God and instead cling to my deep sense of calling—to be wife, mother, *and* minister of the gospel. I felt as though I was mastering the balance beam. The trick was to keep my eyes on a focal point: people who needed love, and the Source behind that love.

We soon discovered that I wasn't the only one struggling with this balance. As our expat community continued to grow, there was an increasing demand for a viable alternative for our children's education. We started looking into starting our own co-op school—and Grace helped make it all possible. She would teach math, art, Bible, and a bit of science to our younger children. The parents would fill in the other spots. After some planning and discussions, we were able to go ahead and rent some rooms in a building that another NGO had vacated. We had nine students in all, ranging from third to eighth grade.

The homeschool co-op was a huge blessing to our kids. The quality of their education improved, and they were able to forge a valuable bond of friendship with other kids who understood the joys and struggles of cross-cultural life. It was beautiful to witness how the Lord would provide for our kids in unexpected ways apart from school. They had the opportunity to learn tae kwon do with a Korean instructor, piano with a Russian woman, and ballet with a French woman. They also learned to play and love soccer from a Brazilian—they were getting a truly international education!

They were developing in other important areas, too. Stephen and I had prayed earnestly from the time of their birth that our children would decide to give their lives to the lordship of Jesus Christ based solely on an understanding of their personal need for a Savior. We weren't sure how and when that would happen, but we trusted God to answer that prayer. Then, as I was having lunch with the kids at the kitchen table one day, one of them brought up the subject of salvation. It was as if a spark had been set off. "I want to be saved," the first one said, and then suddenly all of them wanted to accept the Lord. We all prayed together, and even little Piper joined in, though I knew she didn't quite understand.

Before we'd left the States, we'd been given some wise advice: "Let your kids be part of your ministry life. Let it be *their* lives, too, as much as possible. When they're involved, they won't feel as though they're just along for your ride." We'd done our best to involve the kids in as much of the work as we could. I always tried to take the girls with me to the prison and on other visits whenever possible, and Stephen would often take Joshua with him on his rounds. And we did a lot of visiting as a whole family. Nearly every family had babies and toddlers, and I felt a deep sense of joy as my children played with and loved on the children of these families. My older three certainly missed many things about life in the USA, but they rarely complained.

Even though we didn't fit the mold of the perfect American Christian family, we learned to appreciate our family life outside that box. Together we learned to find real joy in our unusual journey. Simple "happiness" would never have sustained us through the storms that lay ahead.

CHAPTER 9

Faith in the Storms

I HAD JUST HUNG my washing outside when I heard the phone ringing. It was Stephen calling from the other side of town. "Quick!" he said, his voice urgent. "Go look outside. Then be sure and close all the windows right away."

The kids and I hurried up to the roof. In the distance, a solid red wall was advancing our way.

"Whoa! That's so awesome!" Joshua shouted out. The girls took one look and ran back into the house, screaming.

"Hurry, Joshua!" I said urgently. "Help me close all the windows!" We ran back down, slammed all the windows shut, and then I rushed back outside, hoping to rescue my wet clothes off the line. I yanked off the fourth peg and turned to see how much time I still had. And wham! Like a scene from the apocalypse, the sand wall hit me smack in the face, nearly knocking me down and curling its gnarly fingers into my eyes, mouth, ears, and nose. I could hardly breathe. I left my poor sand-offerings on the line and ran inside, trying to expel the red dust from my facial cavities. (I would be sneezing weird brown gunk for days after.)

Despite the early hour, it looked as if it were already dusk outside. We'd experienced sandstorms already at this point, but this one was epic in comparison. The storm came and went in a matter of minutes, leaving behind a fine sand that had found its way through every crack in the house and left a film of dust on every surface. Our white walkway was now indistinguishable from the yard. After about fifteen minutes, a light drizzle graciously came and settled the dust. It was the first "rain" we'd seen all year. It never rained after any of the other sandstorms. The dust would linger in a thick cloud for days.

We faced a lot of storms during our time in this country, both natural and metaphorical. You know that phrase "God will never give you more than you can handle"? It's not true. But do you know what is true? God will never give you more than *he* can handle. We saw that in each and every storm. But some kinds of storms were harder than others.

After surviving our second hot season in the desert, we had made a run for the border for a little vacation—to a little historical town still showing remnants of colonial days in the country south of us. We hoped to catch a bit of a cool-off (and hopefully nothing nasty from the river's insect population).

Being in a different country meant I got to change into a T-shirt and some capris. I felt so free! But by the end of our vacation, my bare legs looked like a ripe strawberry patch. I had been a feast for hundreds of the tiny mosquitos, and I hadn't noticed until it was too late.

On the drive back, the sickness hit. My stomach was churning. My head was in a vise. I was in agony. We were still over a hundred miles from civilization, and all I could do was lie groaning on the back seat for what seemed an eternity, trying not to black out.

My fever was through the roof by the time we got home. We were sure now—I had malaria. Stephen rushed me off to a local clinic. The treatment was the same expensive medicine we had taken faithfully for the prevention of malaria. The prevention regimen—one pill once a week. The treatment— eight pills, two at a time, spread over a twenty-four-hour period. It was almost worse than the sickness. I had psychedelic dreams each time I simply closed my eyes, whether I was sleeping or not. I was so dizzy for the next two weeks that I couldn't climb any stairs or walk from room to room without holding on to the wall.

That was just the first taste of the medical trials to come. Heidi was the next to give us a big scare. We were at our landlady's for a meal one evening, and the after-dinner fruit included some mango, which the kids had never tried before. Heidi put a piece in her mouth and forced a swallow. It was obvious she was not a fan, though the other kids seemed to enjoy it.

That night I was pulled from sleep by a tug on my sleeve. "Mommy . . ."

I switched the light on and sat up with a gasp. Heidi's face was covered in welts.

She complained about her mouth feeling strange, so I got her to wash out her mouth and kept her drinking water through the night, but by morning she was almost unrecognizable. The welts had developed all over her face and body, and she was having trouble breathing. Starting to get scared, we rushed her to a Lebanese doctor in town who we had heard was a believer. He put Heidi on a very strong antihistamine and a steroid.

"It's looking better, Mrs. Foreman," said Dr. Hanna two days later, concern still etched on his face, "but if there is still any sign it is getting worse near her mouth by tomorrow, you must bring her back. Then it is very serious." I was terrified.

During the night, Heidi kept complaining that she couldn't sleep. While Stephen sat up to comfort her, I got on my knees and started seeking the Lord. I'd been doing my best to put on a brave face, but on the inside I was on the verge of a breakdown. I felt utterly helpless. *Here we are in a very underdeveloped country, a thousand miles away from any good hospitals . . . what are we going to do, God?* Of all the fears that had haunted me before we came here, this was at the top of the list.

I tried hard not to let Heidi see my panic. Every few

moments I would inspect her hives and her mouth, and each time it seemed to be getting worse. I tried praying, again, the same exact prayer for Heidi's healing that I had prayed at least a thousand times in the last hour. Finally, at a point of desperation, I just stopped. Then I felt the Lord say, "Listen." That was it. I waited for more, for a miracle, but nothing came.

Then the Holy Spirit led me to Mark 4. Jesus' disciples were terrified in the face of a storm. They were on the verge of certain death, and Jesus lay there sleeping. I had always looked critically at these faithless disciples when I read this story, but suddenly I felt I had no right to criticize. *Lord, why are you sleeping? Why aren't you doing anything?* Then I read the part where Jesus stood up, stretched his hand out to the storm, and said, "Be still."

That was all it took. I sensed him telling me, "I will. I will stand up and say 'Be still' to this. Where is your faith?"

The next morning Heidi woke up feeling perfectly normal. The welts and swelling had completely disappeared. God had again shown himself faithful.

We had to cling to that faithfulness again and again. During one of our vacations, Joshua complained that his leg was hurting as he swam in the hotel pool. At first we assumed he had pulled a muscle in his attempts to do the splits in the water. But later he started running a fever and complaining of a sore throat. We tried unsuccessfully to get his fever down, and by evening he couldn't move his leg because it hurt so much.

Stephen took him into town to see a doctor. Stephen

always wanted to be the one to comfort the kids when they were sick or hurt. It was hard for me to let him take that role, with my maternal instinct kicking me in the guts, but I'm so grateful that he did. He gave his kids those memories of their father being their stronghold in times of distress.

After one look at Joshua, the doctor sent them off to the national hospital in the capital, another four-hour drive away. They couldn't even stop to pick up the girls and me at the hotel. When they arrived, the doctors started prepping Joshua for an appendectomy, but moments before wheeling him into surgery, they suddenly realized that might not be the answer. It took the doctors another day or two to diagnose a staph infection in Joshua's leg—the kind that was often accompanied by pneumonia.

There I was, stranded four hours away from where my nine-year-old son lay ill with pneumonia and a leg infection in a strange hospital room. For eleven excruciating days I hardly got a wink of sleep. I wanted to be with him so badly. Stephen would call each day to update me, and I could hear the concern and exhaustion in his voice. The hardest moment was when he told me that he was only allowed in the room with Joshua during visiting hours.

"What! He's only nine!" I thought I was going to lose it. "They can't isolate my baby like that! You have to make them let you in! He's going to be so traumatized!"

Stephen tried to reassure me. "He's okay, honey. I'm there each day when the doors open for visitation, and I've been taking him treats and making sure they are treating him well." I wasn't satisfied. I was so sure this experience would scar him.

All I could do was cling to God's goodness and ability to work miracles as I spent my days trying to keep the girls occupied and in good spirits. But no matter how hard I tried to keep my composure in front of my girls, I cried every night and prayed and fasted nearly the entire time Joshua was in the hospital. "Please God, please heal my baby. Please don't let the enemy use this experience for his own gain."

It was by God's grace that I didn't know all the details at the time. Joshua had been sharing a room with three other suffering patients, one he described as "skin and bone." He didn't know enough French to communicate much with the nurses. But God graciously protected his mind through all of it. All he talked about were the positive things. Being served coffee every morning . . . Dad bringing him ice cream every day . . . the nice big baobab tree he could see from his window . . . and hearing the helicopter fly overhead that was carrying George Bush on his visit to the capital! I was so taken aback and blessed by how Joshua had responded to the situation, though it had been a torturous one for his dad and me.

The enemy knew my weak spot. From the beginning, I had wrestled with fear in bringing my kids to this place. But God was my children's ultimate protector—I had to remember that. He would always be there, in the midst of every storm, and he would be faithful in any outcome. I just had to keep allowing faith to dictate my life, not fear. This was going to be a continual battle I'd have to fight—but I wasn't alone. God was on my side.

Stephen and I often talked about the dangers and what our decision to come here was really costing us. I made a point of trying to wait up for Stephen on the nights he would go out visiting so we could have some time to "debrief" and pray with each other after the long day, but many nights I was too exhausted. When we saw each other discouraged or tired, we would always try to give encouragement. "We always knew it was going to be hard," we reminded each other. We just had to keep persevering and affirming to ourselves that God had led us here—we just needed to follow him, knowing he was walking with us. With all our strength we held tight to his promise: "Be bold and courageous, for the Lord your God will be with you wherever you go." Being bold and courageous was easier said than done at times, especially when it felt as if God were calling us to be courageous in a war zone, both spiritually and otherwise.

At first I wasn't sure what had woken me. It took a few minutes for my sleepy brain to realize that a plane was flying somewhere overhead.

I rolled over to look at the clock. It was 1:00 a.m. I looked out the window. A military plane was circling the city. Stephen hadn't woken up yet, and I lay back down for a few minutes. Then . . .

BOOM.

An anti-aircraft missile? Stephen woke with a jolt. "What's going on?"

"Sounds like the city is under attack. Should we go up to the roof and check it out?"

We hurried up to the roof, still barefoot. Everyone else in the neighborhood had the same idea. It looked like the commotion was coming from the presidential palace, which was only about two or three miles away.

"Are you all okay?" a neighbor yelled over to us. He was holding a phone to his ear.

"Yes, we're fine. But what's going on?" Stephen called back.

Our neighbor shook his head. "We think the presidential palace is under attack."

We were witnessing a coup d'état. We heard the rattling of machine guns in the distance. More explosions rattled the house.

The shots were getting closer.

This is going to traumatize our kids! I thought to myself as we went back inside to take cover. When we checked on the kids, we were amazed that they were still asleep. "It's impossible that they are sleeping through this!" Stephen whispered as we closed the door to the girls' room.

Soon tanks were rolling through the streets in the distance. It was frightening and fascinating at the same time. We didn't know what might happen. The current president had taken power by coup d'état twenty years earlier. He wasn't a tyrant, but our country certainly wasn't a democracy.

The next day, we learned what had happened. The

president had been ousted and exiled by his military general. The entire city was in confusion. Some walked the streets, cheering that the president they disliked was out of office. Others were scared out of their wits and refused to come out of their homes. The US embassy told us to stay indoors until the situation calmed down.

For whatever reason, the opposition had decided to set all the prisoners loose from the main prison. Several hundred convicted men, many of them thieves, ran free in the city. In the week that followed, almost every house in our neighborhood was robbed.

We prayed in faith that the new leadership would rule justly, bring security, and truly serve the people of our nation. Once the turmoil had settled, they put word out that if the prisoners came back voluntarily they would not be punished for leaving—but that if they were caught, there would be dire consequences. Most of the men did turn themselves in, eventually. But for a while after the coup, everybody was on edge.

"Do not come to the training center tomorrow. There is a plan to attack you after the Friday prayers."

A few days into getting the first few classes set up at our newly launched training center, one of our newest and most energetic team members, a Brazilian, brought some local boys up to the balcony of our training center to discuss ideas for the soccer program. The men at the mosque across the way saw them and started yelling across the rooftops at our team member. Rumors about Westerners had circulated the city for years, and no matter how ridiculous a rumor might be, it seemed people believed everything they heard. Perhaps it was leftover resentment and distrust from the colonialist era. One of the craziest rumors I heard was, "Americans offer local children candy to coax them to the beach, and then they eat them." And another rumor that very well may have fueled the anger of our devout Muslim neighbors in the mosque was, "Americans will give children candy with Jesus' face on it to entice them to convert to Christianity."

Later that week, someone in the community told Stephen and Timothy about the impending attack.

"Why do they want to attack us?" Stephen's brow furrowed.

The man shook his head. "I just know they had a meeting at the mosque and they are going to attack you."

"Okay," Stephen said thoughtfully. "But tomorrow I will be here."

The next day, Stephen, Timothy, and Ali waited inside the training center. Sure enough, following the afternoon prayers, the imam and a large number of men from the mosque came with stones to attack them. They banged on the door screaming, "*Allah hu akbar!*"

Stephen walked the down the steps and opened the door. He calmly greeted the men in their own language, and suddenly the man who started the riot calmed the crowd and told Stephen, "We are listening."

As Stephen explained who we were and what we were out

to accomplish, the crowd remained calm. The police ordered Stephen and the imam to the station to file a report. Stephen offered him a ride to the station and continued to explain that we were there to help their community by providing vocational training.

"Above all," he said, "we are following Christ's most important command of loving Allah with all our heart, soul, mind, and strength and loving our neighbors as ourselves. You are our neighbors, and we love you."

"We thought you were coming here to convert our young people," the imam confessed.

Stephen smiled. "We have no intention of converting your children. Only Allah has the power to do that." And just like that, a bond of friendship was forged from peace in the face of conflict.

That evening, we found encouragement from the words of Jesus in John 15:20-21:

> Remember what I told you: "A servant is not greater than his master." If they persecuted me, they will persecute you also. They will treat you this way because of my name, for they do not know the one who sent me.

Many of the locals also offered us kind words and made it clear that they did not condone what had happened. It didn't take long for us to see that God was in fact working the situation for good. The incident had not only strengthened our faith and the unity among our team but had also solidified our presence in the neighborhood—more people were coming to us and showing interest in what we were doing.

And incredibly, that imam became an advocate for us. When the landlord for the training center decided to significantly increase our rent a couple of years later, which would have forced us to relocate, the imam immediately stepped in and pressured the landlord to keep our rent reasonable. He told the landlord that we were benefiting their community and it would be absurd to make us leave. The landlord finally negotiated, and we stayed. Several of the imam's family members and even others from the mosque sought training from our facility. We would have never imagined that the Lord could turn such a scary, hate-filled situation into a beautiful friendship!

CHAPTER 10

Talking about Jesus

OUR TRAINING CENTER WAS THRIVING. We provided French-literacy, computer-literacy, and business classes. The business program became a prerequisite for our microcredit candidates so that the people would have a solid foundation of money management, accountability, and good business practices. Existing cooperatives were encouraged to take the classes to further their skills.

The soccer program, despite being the cause of some ruffled feathers, developed into a great success. The patch of thorny, litter-strewn ground we'd painstakingly fashioned into a soccer field became a magnet for boys of all ages to come to show off and improve their "football" skills. And they weren't the only ones. Heidi and Joshua were right alongside them, getting dirty and bruised and loving it.

The center also solved the problem of our overflowing sewing classes, allowing for two or three different classes a week where we could provide one-on-one training. Those classes meant we could let the women practice individually on electric sewing machines, enabling them to start making clothes of a professional selling standard—a trade monopolized by men at that point.

Attendees were charged a small fee to cover the rent and salaries of the locals we had employed so that it could become self-sustaining while remaining nonprofit. This also encouraged a sense of dignity and of motivation to follow through on the training. And of course there was grace for those who struggled. The support from various embassies and organizations enabled us to provide a fair amount of loans and scholarships. Within its first few months, the center had around 120 students.

Apart from the educational benefits, the center had allowed us to provide jobs for several people in teaching and assistant positions. Stephen had staffed the center with local talent as much as he could. He had an amazing gift of discernment in his leadership. Ali was the perfect "right-hand man." Timothy, Stephen's coworker in the prison ministry, fell in as Stephen's second-in-command. These men were worth their weight in gold. Stephen gave a lot of input and guidance in the beginning, training them both as leaders.

Stephen had hired our good friend Amir to do follow-up

visits and monthly payment collections with the cooperatives. As a child, Amir had been greatly influenced by two single Canadian women who had come to his country to teach children. He had been drawn to their love and kindness to the children, and especially to this Jesus they were constantly talking about. The women were expelled after two years in the country for teaching the children Bible stories and songs and telling them about Jesus.

Many years later, Amir came into contact with other Christians while traveling in another country. The seeds planted in Amir's heart years earlier began to sprout as his new Christian friends shared the Good News with him. Amir gladly committed his life to following Christ, though he was very discreet about his faith to avoid persecution. He did his work faithfully, and Stephen began meeting with him regularly to disciple him.

Amir's wife, Jameila, had not yet chosen to follow Christ, and this was a burden for Amir. He also struggled with the conflicting message his sons would be receiving from parents with two different faiths. I was delighted when Jameila enrolled for sewing classes at the center, and we immediately became good friends.

By the end of the year, we were thrilled to have our first nine students graduate from sewing class. We tried to make the event as special for them as possible, inviting them to our house for a change of setting. We decorated and stocked up with lots of food, tea, and soda. Phoebe and I gave a speech to honor and congratulate these dear women, and we encouraged them to continue growing and utilizing their skills and talents. Then we called each woman up to shake her hand, take her picture, and hand her a little diploma certificate we'd had framed. We had never seen such big smiles from them. The diploma also qualified them to apply for a small business loan and a sewing machine, and in the months that followed, many of them joined together to form successful cooperatives.

Jameila was at the top of the class. Her work was unparalleled, and so was her character. We were delighted when she earned her own sewing machine. She was beside herself as she oohed and aahed over her new gift. This machine would enable her to make quality clothes for her family and to generate income from the items she would sell. Amir complained that Jameila's cooking had become a little less than extraordinary now that her days were filled with sewing. We told Jameila about "the wife of noble character" in Proverbs 31, emphasizing that her excellent work ethic was reflected in her housekeeping as well as in her sewing. Their small two-room block house was rugged and bare, but it was the cleanest I'd seen in the country. We also affirmed the loving care she poured out on her children and Amir. Amir couldn't argue with that.

Phoebe and I started visiting Jameila regularly. Thankfully I now felt that I could hold a decent conversation in the local Arabic dialect, and Phoebe, whose language ability was surpassing mine, was a huge help. We enjoyed many hours of profound conversations with Jameila. During one of our visits, the Holy Spirit prompted me to ask her whether she'd be interested in studying the teachings of Jesus.

She was thoughtful for a moment, then smiled. "Oh yes. I'd be happy to," she said. Though she been taught from a young age that Jesus was a wonderful prophet, Jameila knew nothing of his life, miracles, and teachings. Although she was from the lower classes, Jameila was very intelligent and had made the most of her limited schooling. She could read quite well and had a good understanding of the materials we were covering. She loved reading the stories from the Arabic New Testament we'd given her and then retelling the stories to us in the local dialect to show her understanding and to ask questions. And Jameila gradually fell in love with the Jesus of the Bible. We led her through a seven-part teaching called "The Seven Commands of Christ," which ended with an opportunity to accept or reject the teaching.

"Do you believe what you've been reading?" we asked Jameila.

Without a moment's hesitation she replied, "Yes, of course!" as though there was never a doubt.

There was no clear point during our meetings with her at which she had distinctly said yes to following Christ. It had been a process—which challenged our Western mind-set of what it means to be "saved." I grew up believing that the ticket to salvation was the "salvation prayer." Repeat after the evangelist, and eureka! You're in. God was using Jameila to broaden my perspective and break out of the American Christian box in which I had carried him my whole life. In teaching Jameila who Christ is, we were discipling her right into the Kingdom without realizing it.

Soon afterward, Jameila expressed her desire to be baptized. And if that weren't enough cause for joy, our daughter Heidi also asked to be baptized. We didn't go to the beach very often—it was, after all, a hassle to clean five gallons of sand out of the car every time; and even our four-wheel-drive car would inevitably get stuck in the sand trying to cross the dunes, and we would have to dig ourselves out—but it was the ideal place for such a special occasion. We went on a mild day with fairly calm waves. This part of the beach was clean and quiet and hadn't been developed for the public at all. There was no natural shelter—the beach was simply where the dunes met the water—so we brought along a nomad-style tent for protection from the sun. Together, Stephen and Amir baptized Heidi, then Amir baptized his wife. We were overjoyed to see our precious daughter take this huge step of obedience, and as we watched Jameila take the same step, we felt as if we were witnessing the book of Acts come to life.

Jameila's education and intelligence had helped pave an easier road to her accepting the truth. While the Holy Spirit is no respecter of education or intellect, we did find that in this society, education seemed to play a role in people's receptivity. In Islam, religion or spirituality is primarily the man's domain, because it ties in so closely with education and intellectualism. A lot of the women in our country were quite uneducated, which meant they didn't learn as much of the Qur'an. Their primary role was taking care of the household, not engaging in intellectual debates. As we shared with women, we found this to be both a negative and a positive. On one hand, they seemed less bound by the theology of Islam, but on the other hand, spirituality was a priority for them. It was part of their identity. Being Muslim was the life they were born into; it was not a matter of choice. They did their prayers faithfully and smacked their kids if they weren't praying right, but beyond going through the motions, theology and apologetics were not their business. Those like Jameila who were a little more educated would show a bit more interest in discussing the Qur'an and its teachings compared to the Bible, but they were few and far between. Trying to guide our conversations so I could defend my beliefs and faith had led only to uncomfortable confrontation. Theological discussions were a challenge to have with most of the women.

But it was easy to interject stories about Jesus into conversation.

"Did you hear that so-and-so has a secret relationship with so-and-so and she isn't married?" Someone would be nudging a co-conspirator. "She should be locked up for shaming her family that way!"

"You know," I'd mention, "that reminds me of a story Jesus told . . ." The door was wide open to share about the woman caught in adultery and how Jesus had forgiven her (John 8:1-11). I was simply telling a story. And they were always mesmerized. Looking back, I realize that we were also modeling this same effective tool to Fatu and the other believing women.

Stories were also a great key in our multilingual study groups, where some of the women were illiterate. It was difficult to keep the studies going in all the different languages, but with stories we could be more creative in our methods. Phoebe would tell the story, Fatu would repeat it in the local tribal language, and Zaina would tell it in the local Arab dialect; and we'd go around until each woman had repeated it in her own language. Those who had a grasp of more than one language could correct the others.

Afterward we would challenge the women to go and tell the story to at least one person that week, whether a family member or friend. The next week we'd encourage them to share how it went. This helped us bypass the barriers of both illiteracy and culture. It finally felt as if we were at least in the ballpark of success in reaching our friends.

Each time we felt we were making progress, we'd be tempted to look over our shoulder to where we'd just sowed, anxiously searching for signs of fruit . . . but the results seemed too few. One week a friend would seem interested, and the next she would be completely against even discussing spiritual things. Some days the battle against discouragement was overwhelming. *Are we doing this right? Are we doing enough?*

During those times of questioning I struggled to really love the people, and many times I simply lost the desire to even be there. I was weak. I was homesick. Some nights I would lie awake, too frustrated and discouraged to sleep. At times like these, it wasn't particularly easy to "love my neighbor as myself."

One hot afternoon—probably after one such sleepless night—I was washing dishes in the kitchen, thinking about making a long-overdue visit to one of our neighbors around the corner. This particular family had taken a real interest in us and were very easy to share life and faith with. Unlike in my visits with other women, faith was a constant topic of conversation with this family. The mother had made it her life's mission to convert me to Islam, and I had found myself growing tired of resisting and debating and trying to convince her that she was wrong and needed to convert to my faith because it is truth. Because of her persistence in trying to prove me wrong, my love for this family had grown cold. And I had no desire to go and see them.

I was tired. It was hot outside, and we hadn't seen the blue sky through the haze of dust for days. I hadn't been feeling very perky for some time.

I stood there for a few minutes, trying to muster up a spark of enthusiasm to make the visit. I was struggling with the guilt of letting my friends and God down. I could just make the decision to visit out of duty, but I didn't want to be a righteous robot. I wanted to be real, sincere.

Then it dawned on me. I needed to ask God for his love for them. He had promised to supply all our needs, and I was in major need of a good dose of love to share. So I prayed, *Lord, you know how annoyed I get by things. You know I can't* stomach the goat milk they will serve tonight. You know I'm tired and I'll have to force a smile. I know I should go and see them because I need to be a good friend, but I just can't do it . . . Please, give me a love for them. Give me your love for them. Just wash over me with what you feel for them.

And then I sensed him pierce my heart with his reply. "What do you think I feel when Zarah prays to me? Or when she does the ritual washing before those prayers? Do you think it angers me when she prostrates herself in prayer? Do you think it angers me to hear her say that I am the greatest and there are no other gods?"

I was bewildered. I assumed that all of my Muslim friends were just unbelievers who blatantly resisted the truth, and I had come to my own conclusions of what was in my friend's heart. But I was deeply touched when I considered my Father's heart as he watched my dear friend and her tireless and sincere efforts to do everything she thought he expected of her—with faithfulness that would put my obedience to shame. I hadn't given much thought to how God felt about all the efforts and commitment of Muslims based on their understanding of their Creator. As I realized this, I felt that God injected a dose of his love for the people into my hardened heart. My friend had no idea that her Creator longed to redeem her and extend the grace and salvation he had provided through the perfect sacrifice of his Son, Jesus Christ. And because of my own misunderstanding, I had allowed bitterness to take root. I felt like a repentant child who had been reprimanded.

Suddenly I found myself prostrate on the kitchen floor, sobbing uncontrollably. The emotion was beyond anything I could have ever mustered up. "God, I'm so sorry! I've been leaning on my own understanding, and on my own strength. It's not enough, I need yours!" As I began to collect my whirling thoughts, I sensed a floodlight come on in my clouded mind. I could do nothing in my own strength. And God didn't expect me to. I had been trying to live out my faith through my flesh instead of his Spirit. Like a needle with no thread, all I can do alone is poke holes through the fabric of others' lives—but with the divine thread securely attached, I can weave God's love and power in and out of the lives of others, allowing the Lord to mend and heal and bring everything together for his glory. I just simply need to submit, stitch by stitch, until the grand tapestry of his design is complete.

This realization wasn't a one-time thing. I had to keep submitting, keep asking, keep dying daily to myself and my flesh and allowing God's Spirit to live and work through me. Many times when I went to visit someone, I'd start off feeling aloof and unconcerned, and I had to ask the Lord again to set the tone for his Holy Spirit to work through me, to keep breaking my heart for these people and helping me fall in love with their country.

Trust me: Submission like this isn't always easy, but the more we invite God to love through us, the more he answers our prayers. He certainly continued to answer mine, to the point where my heart wanted to burst with my love for the people and an appreciation for their sincere commitment to God—or at least their understanding of him.

It can be so tempting to strive to achieve the transformation we hope to see in others. Stephen and I were wearing down, overcomplicating the simplicity of the message of the Kingdom and in the process losing our joy in God's call. Then the Lord gave us a simple solution:

Stop striving. All I need you to do is love them.

How had we lost sight of that simple guideline? All we needed to do was follow God's two basic commands: *Love the Lord your God with all your heart, soul, mind, and strength—and love your neighbor as yourself.* It didn't matter if we had the right points, the right arguments, the right "evangelism style." There was no perfect formula. Christ had brought us here so we could be agents of his love and blessing to these people.

Of course we didn't ignore strategy altogether—there's wisdom in planning, and we discovered that certain methods seemed to bring more fruit. But like the apostle Paul wrote, we could speak with the tongues of angels, but if we didn't do everything from a starting point of love, we'd be nothing better than clanging cymbals. Embracing this truth brought such peace and freedom. We had to come to terms with the fact that sharing the love of Christ didn't belong in a category or slot on our calendar. It was a lifestyle that summed up our purpose on earth. As long as we were loving God and loving the people around us, we'd stay on track. God was refreshing our eyes to see a little more clearly what he sees. We saw the crowds of people in our city differently now, and we were moved more than ever with compassion.

And we were beginning to understand our mission and what it would cost us. To love our neighbor as ourselves meant opening not only the door of our home to them but also the door to our lives. This would cost us our time and maybe our comfort and security. It seemed too radical, but did Christ in his ministry on earth do any less?

CHAPTER 11

Urgency

"YOU'RE THE FIRST WHITE PERSON I've ever met who makes it a point to share about his religious beliefs. Most white people I've talked to avoid the subject as if it means nothing to them."

One of our friends said those words to Stephen one day. It shook us. What was the legacy we Westerners had been leaving in these dark places? Hollywood. Colonialism. Junk food. Oil rigs. Wars. This had been the extent of Western generosity. Why were we so reticent to share the greatest gift of all—one that would last beyond celebrity romances, political promises, and junk food? Why were we allowing Coca-Cola bottles to reach the most obscure places, but not the very Word of God?

Stephen began feeling a real sense of urgency about getting the Good News out. "The gospel is only good news if it gets there in time," he would say. He started getting his hands on all the Bible-based materials he could find in all of the languages in our country. We'd hand out Bibles and see them being sold in the market a few days later, but we could only laugh—all the better for circulation! We held on to the passage in Isaiah that the Word would not return void but would accomplish God's desires and achieve the purpose for which he sent it.

A young man named Zayd showed us just how true that scripture is. Zayd had met Stephen through a mutual friend whom Stephen had just started discipling. Zayd was an intelligent young man, but all he wanted to do was argue. One day while we were visiting Zayd's family, I heard what sounded like a parliamentary debate going on in the next room. At home later, Stephen and I talked about whether this was a relationship we should pursue. Should we just cut ties and move on? Debates were almost always a dead end, and they weren't a good use of Stephen's limited time. But as we prayed it through, Stephen felt convicted that he should persevere with Zayd.

I had my doubts. "Are you sure you're not wasting your time?" I pleaded. "It seems to me that his only goal is to prove you wrong, and I can't stand his arrogance!"

Stephen, as always, was calm and assured. "I don't understand why. I just feel like the Lord is telling me to be patient with him, and not to turn him away."

The visits became more frequent. I was amazed at Stephen's unwillingness to allow his patience and joy to be stolen by Zayd's heated defense of Islam. Even in his own defense, Stephen managed to overcome the debate with a sincere love for this new friend. Zayd would leave laughing and embracing Stephen while spouting out blessings in Arabic over our family. Zayd constantly pursued Stephen—and slowly, his debates turned into questions. Stephen enjoyed the lighter atmosphere of their visits, and eventually he gave Zayd a copy of the Gospel of Luke.

After a pleasant visit one evening, Zayd announced that he was leaving to travel to one of the northern cities for a while for work. Stephen gave the typical blessings in the local language and bid him farewell. And then, the day before his departure, Zayd showed up at our front door with a strange new look in his eyes.

"I had a dream last night," he said, his eyes wide. "This man in bright white was standing before me. I think it was Jesus. His arms were loaded with loaves of bread, and he gave them to me. As I looked at the bread I saw the word *Luke* written on them. He told me I must take this bread to give to my friends in the city I'm traveling to. You are the only one I know that has a book of Luke. Please, do you have any more you can give?"

Stephen was taken aback by Zayd's demeanor. It was as if he'd seen a ghost. "Yes, of course, come in." Stephen spent a few moments with Zayd, processing his dream. It was unclear where Zayd was in his faith that day, but it was clearly a milestone in a process put into motion by the "man in bright white." Stephen offered to pray for him and his journey in Jesus' name, an offer Zayd eagerly accepted.

It made sense that God would choose to speak to Zayd through a dream. Muslims take dreams very seriously. God was working in a miraculous way. As promised, his Word would not return to him void—and he would even use a Muslim to get it out!

After returning from his trip, Zayd came to visit Stephen a few times and they began studying the Word together. It was clear he'd had a change of attitude. After some further deep discussions, he made his decision to follow Christ.

Stephen was inspired. He never left the house without Bibles and materials and was always ready to share the Good News with anyone he crossed paths with. He didn't hesitate or feel concerned about what people might say or think. He simply shared his heart with a smile. He wasn't threatening anyone. He wasn't forcing his religion on anyone. He was simply living out his faith in the same way he would if he were in the USA. He was obvious. To him, clandestine Christianity was an oxymoron.

Not all Christian workers in our context agreed with our excessive openness with our faith. One day, a team member named Seth rode to our house with Stephen. Stephen immediately sparked up a friendly conversation with the taxi driver, and by the time they reached our house the taxi driver and Stephen were like the best of friends.

As Stephen and Seth were getting out of the taxi, Stephen

asked the driver if he would like a cassette tape with stories of Jesus. The man gladly accepted and drove away.

Once inside the house, Seth came unglued. "What were you thinking, Stephen? Not only does that man know you are sharing the gospel, now he knows where you live! Doesn't that make you afraid for your safety? And what about the safety of your family?"

Stephen waited until Seth had finished, then replied calmly, "Seth, I understand your concern. But think about it—we may be the only true Christians that man will ever meet."

Stephen encouraged everyone on our team to be bold and seize the moment—and to not let fear steal what might be that one chance to reach someone and save a soul for eternity.

"Are we transferring fear to our new brothers and sisters by valuing security above the gospel and living a lifestyle of 'safety first'?" he would ask them. "Nowhere in the message of Jesus Christ does fear have a place. Wouldn't we be contaminating the message of Christ if we allow our own fear to dictate our level of obedience to God? It seems to me that we can't encourage boldness unless we first exemplify it ourselves."

Fear was one of the major spiritual strongholds over the nation. We prayed against it constantly. And fear was definitely one of the biggest roadblocks to the growth of the small community of local believers—and for good reason. Christians in closed countries like this suffered persecution of which we know nothing in America. In this country there were only two choices: Be a Muslim—or risk the loss of your job, your family, and potentially your life. Of course our friends were afraid. But we knew that the church would not grow until they were willing to push forward in the face of persecution—not out of recklessness, but as wise as serpents and gentle as doves. Out of love for God and those around them.

We tried to inspire our friends, but though we faced our own fair share of fears and risks and even hardships, our reality was very different. We at least had the full backing of our family and supporters back home—and we were free to be Christians in America *and* in the Muslim world. It was one thing to talk about being bold and courageous in face of persecution, but did we have any real authority on the subject? How could we model this principle when we weren't personally faced with being disowned by our parents or losing our means of feeding our children? Encouragement would only go so far—God would have to stir his people to boldness.

We didn't have peace about the persecution of our local brothers and sisters. We knew it was inevitably going to be difficult for them, but was their only choice in following Jesus to disassociate with their family and lose their cultural identity? How would the light spread that way? Wasn't God just as passionate about redeeming their families? Even in the midst of persecution, the persecutors may be the opposition, but they are not the enemy. There had to be a way for our friends to stay in their context and follow Christ without outright dishonoring their families. These were the questions that consumed our conversation and prayers many nights as we lay in our quiet room, unable to sleep.

We weren't blind to the fact that the more we stepped out to take ground, the more attention we'd be drawing to ourselves—and not just the good kind.

"I equate evangelism with terrorism," the minister of religious affairs in a neighboring country had said. Fortunately our local government didn't seem quite as extreme—rather, they were indifferent to the news that a handful of people in the city had converted to Christianity. One day, a friend of Stephen's who worked for the government came to him and said, "We know what you're doing. We know why you're here. But we want you to stay because we appreciate the good work you're doing for our country. Just please be careful."

But the government's tolerant attitude infuriated the Muslim extremist minority and a few individuals in the police department, who took it upon themselves to harass people. We could curry favor with the government all we liked and try to create a positive and loving image, but as Stephen's dad had pointed out from the beginning, it only takes one to wreak deadly havoc.

CHAPTER 12

Blessed Are the Balanced

STEPHEN'S NEW FERVENCY in ministry began to take a toll on our family life. I had always been incredibly blessed to have Stephen by my side as my best friend and pillar of support. I was convinced that our marriage was rock-solid and couldn't ever be shaken. This Islamic country was known for its high divorce rate, and we wanted to set an example in a place of such brokenness. One of the biggest highlights of my life was loving Stephen and being loved by him, serving him and serving with him. He loved his children, he loved his family, and he loved Muslims. And above all, he loved his Savior. Anything that fell outside of those categories held no appeal for him. After several years, he came up with his own beatitude: "Blessed are the balanced." He'd come to value that proper balance in ministry, family, work, and community responsibility was needed for a healthy life.

But at this point, as our work and ministry kicked up a few notches, we were beginning to lose that blessed balance. Our relationships and family life seemed to be under attack as work and ministry commitments swallowed up Stephen's time and energy like quicksand. Stephen wanted to have integrity in terms of doing what we said we were there to do, so he was intentional about putting in forty hours a week of NGO work. But that meant the deeper, more focused visits had to take place after-hours. Stephen didn't take either task lightly, and both were very time-consuming and energy draining. He was overextending himself. Some days he'd come home after the kids were in bed, and we hadn't seen anything of him the whole day. He always tried to be home in time for dinner, but often he wouldn't make it. Not only was *he* coming home to leftovers, but it also sometimes felt as if the kids and I had to settle for leftovers. It seemed we were getting the "love your neighbors" thing right, and we were seeing fruit as a result. More and more people were drawn to Stephen, and I began observing my kids competing for his attention.

At first, I wrote it off as simply a matter of priorities. I tried to ignore the feeling that I, too, was slipping down his priority list, but the truth kept sneaking out through my attitude. There was a tension in our marriage unlike anything we'd ever experienced. I would try to express my concern, asking him to be around a little more, but my pleas came out as sarcasm because it felt as if he weren't hearing me.

I had never been tempted to question his love for us before. Where were these thoughts coming from that were haunting my mind? I began to have difficulty sleeping. I sensed a new sin crouching at my door, a new fear. But how was I to master this one? Was it even possible? Even my prayers became bitter: "He gave up his job and all his possessions for your sake; are you asking him to give up his family, too, God?"

Late one night we were having yet another conversation on the issue that just seemed to be going around in circles . . . until I said, "You know, we're your neighbors too." Stephen just sat in silence. Hurt and frustration began welling up inside me, and just as the words "I give up" were just about to blast out of my mouth like a cannonball, a voice inside pierced my heart: *Enough*. I took my cue and walked out of the room. I went up to the roof and sat down, leaning my head back and staring at the vast desert sky.

"God, I don't know what to do anymore. I don't know what to say that will change his heart and make him see," I sobbed.

The more I prayed, the more I felt the Holy Spirit saying, *Be quiet. Listen.* So I sat there staring into the sky until the tears slowed and my breathing calmed.

A Scripture popped into mind out of the blue. *Do not fear! Stand by and see the salvation of the LORD which He will accomplish for you today. . . . The LORD will fight for you while you keep silent* (Exodus 14:13-14, NASB). Like the Israelites running from the Egyptians, I felt as if the enemy were hot on our trail in our marriage and gaining ground by the second. I didn't see an escape, and I was afraid. The words *Do not fear . . . keep silent* repeated over and over in my spirit.

Suddenly, out of nowhere, I started feeling a strange, deep conviction in my own heart: I had been pointing my finger in the wrong direction. I finally gave in: "Father, I don't understand, but I'm all in. I'm committed to you, and I'm commitment to Stephen. No matter what."

I relinquished my rights to have a perfect marriage and a perfect family. Then it happened. As if my lenses were once again being refocused, I began to see things more clearly. I realized that I had been holding an American standard of family over Stephen's head and expecting him to submit. When I was a stay-at-home mom back in North Carolina, I would listen faithfully to programs about family on Christian radio—about the list of nonnegotiable things that a dad must do to nurture and protect his relationship with his wife and his children. And I had bought into the illusion that if those requirements weren't met, then the marriage would fail and the children would inevitably make bad life decisions. I couldn't reconcile the standard of a perfect American family with the standard of a thriving ministry. One or the other would have to be compromised.

I sat up there half the night. I still didn't know what the solution was, but I had hope for the first time. I left the roof that night with a deep sense of peace, offering God a blank slate and asking him to show me his picture of what our family was supposed to be. And incredibly, as I lay there finally dozing off, I was overcome with a renewed love and passion for this incredible man God had blessed me with. Stephen was the most God-fearing, loving, and selfless man I had ever known. He was mine, and I was his. I rolled over and snuggled his warm sleeping body. A deep and indescribable comfort washed over me as I drifted off.

A couple of days later, while playing a board game with the kids, I had an epiphany. When Stephen walked in late that night with a tired smile, I was eager to share my idea with him. He walked over and wrapped me in a hug. I sighed and let myself relax in his arms for a few moments.

"So, this loving my family as my neighbor thing . . ." Stephen paused. "Any more ideas on application?"

I smiled up at him. He had been listening after all. "Well, yeah, actually. I think God gave me the answer this afternoon."

My enthusiasm piqued his interest. "Awesome. Well, what's the answer?"

"Family night," I said firmly. "Once a week. A night that the kids know they can look forward to having your undivided attention. We'll have dinner together, and we'll play games or watch a movie."

"Oh really?" He pulled me back in for another hug.

"I think it could really help, Stephen. Just one night a week, all to ourselves. No phone calls. No doorbells. No meetings."

"Well, I don't agree with that at all."

I pulled back and eyed him questioningly. He was grinning.

"It needs to be at least *two* nights a week! And even more as often as we can." Stephen folded me back into a bear hug. "It's a wonderful idea, my love. I think we have our answer."

It was a simple one. But it worked, as simple solutions usually do—especially God-given ones. Apart from giving us all something to look forward to for the week, it immediately brought that crucial balance back into our lives. We would never reach the "perfect family" status by American standards, but we were deeply content.

Not only was Stephen jealously committed to our family night, but he began running the kids around to many of their other activities so he could have the extra time with them. I honestly don't know how he managed to fit everything in—it just didn't seem humanly possible to be so many things to so many people. But God enabled him. Our marriage, friendship, and intimacy flourished as never before. My prayers for him intensified, and so did my appreciation. I fell deeper and deeper in love with him.

Heidi had been feeling a bit isolated with no Christian friends her age—most of the other Western kids had already gone off to the boarding school. She asked whether we'd pray about sending her to a Christian boarding school for high school. The idea had come as quite a blow at first. We'd been going through so much as a family, and this was going to be a big adjustment. But as we prayed, we felt a peace about it. We dreaded the separation, but we were happy for Heidi, knowing she would be in the Lord's hands and have the tremendous blessing of being in a good Christian school.

Stephen and I certainly didn't take for granted the privilege of choosing our children's education. We often talked with our local friends who were following Christ about the difficulties they faced in their kids' schooling. In the local schools the classrooms were packed to bursting, often with less than one teacher per classroom, and education was naturally dominated by a Muslim worldview. All children, whether they went to regular school or not, were also sent to small neighborhood schools where they were taught the Qur'an. Meanwhile, our friends were trying to teach their kids about Christ at home, and the teachers were catching on that something was different. They'd even started harassing the kids and hitting them over the head with a stick if they didn't recite the Qur'an properly. The conflict was a huge burden for these parents, and the topic of much prayer and fasting.

We were thrilled to see our own kids developing into young men and women of God, and we knew beyond a doubt that he had big plans for them. As "third-culture kids," they faced very different challenges than most, and we prayed that God would enable us to faithfully and selflessly do our part in their mental, emotional, and spiritual growth.

Joshua and Ellie, now just hitting adolescence, had mentioned a few times their wish to be baptized, but we had decided to hold off until Heidi had a break from school. Our baptism service would include one of Fatu's daughters, who had just given her life to follow Christ, along with our beautiful young friend Mouna from sewing class.

The scene was a glorious family celebration. Stephen and I baptized our son and daughter in the sparkling waves, and then Phoebe and I baptized our two daughters-in-Christ. We imagined the Son smiling down on us, his children. Fatu broke out in a worship song in the local language, and we all joined in, singing and dancing along the sand. After we'd joined hands in prayer, we stood and gazed over the rumbling sea, in awe of the greatness of our God. Fatu looked at us, then turned to face the vast desert. "Look at this country." She gestured before us. "God has given us this land, and we must take it for him!" We turned our faces to the great span of North Africa and considered the huge task ahead of us. The ground was hard, the land scorched and unyielding. But beside us, we had each other, and a promise from God in Isaiah 35:1: "The wilderness and the desert will be glad, and the Arabah will rejoice and blossom" (NASB).

All the stress that Stephen had been dealing with over the past year had taken its toll on him emotionally, mentally, and physically. But he'd keep telling people, "What doesn't kill you makes you stronger." I kept praying for the *latter* outcome.

Once again our ministry work was shifting up a gear as

we launched a second training center in a different area of town, catering to people who had a hard time getting to the main center. Stephen had trained up his protégés well enough by this point to hand them near sole responsibility for running the main center. In addition, Elsa, the co-leader of our NGO, had started an Arabic literacy project on the southern outskirts of the city. We were also excited that our new collaboration with the US embassy and the local ministry of justice on confronting the issue of human trafficking.

If we hadn't already implemented our family nights, I don't know where Stephen would have fit us in. But he made sure to keep family a priority. Times when Heidi was back home were always special, and we looked forward to her next summer holiday with us. By now Joshua had received his acceptance letter to boarding school and would be starting in the fall.

That Father's Day was a special time for Stephen and the kids. Heidi was home for summer break, and the kids wanted to go out for milkshakes. Money was always tight, and we hardly ever splurged; but Stephen would indulge the kids once in a while, though he'd never order any treats for himself. So for Father's Day, the kids were determined to take Stephen to one of the nicest restaurants in the city—a classy place frequented mainly by the elite with air-conditioning, pristine marble, beautiful furniture, Persian carpets, and a pricey menu to go along with all of it. To their delight, Stephen not only agreed to go but also ordered himself a chocolate milkshake! I stayed so they could have their dad all to themselves. I was so glad he'd spent that extra time with the kids that weekend. Every spare moment Stephen had was invested in the kids and me; it seemed it was the icing on the cake for his day. We took a lot of walks, played a lot of games. It all seemed too surreal compared to where we had been only months earlier. I was so thankful for the memories being made that Father's Day. I just didn't know how thankful I would soon be that they'd spent such rich time together.

CHAPTER 13

Enemy Territory

THE NEWS WAS GRIM. Several European tourists had been attacked by a group of terrorists near a small town 150 miles south of the capital. The terrorists had killed four of them and seriously injured the others before stealing their car. Within a few days, the local authorities arrested five suspects from an extremist group linked to al-Qaeda, but somehow two of them escaped from prison on the day of their trial. The police ended up chasing them right through our neighborhood. We heard gunfire and later learned that the police had cornered the men in someone's house and shot them there, killing one.

Everyone interviewed in the media disowned the violence, insisting that it had been an isolated incident and was not a reflection of their people or the state. "Our country is a peaceful country," they maintained. Although we knew this to be true, others around the world were not convinced.

After the murders, the various embassies started heightening security, and some other terrorists were arrested. The fact that al-Qaeda did have a presence in the country was a little more real to us now. We had always been on our guard security-wise, but the last few months' events had put us on high alert. We made sure to change our routes from time to time and not put ourselves in any vulnerable situations.

We were sensing more danger in our work, too. Stephen had met a young man named Malak who seemed very interested in the gospel. Malak was in his twenties and was married to a girl who looked no more than fifteen. They were very poor and had just had a baby. She had no idea what she was doing as a mother, but their little baby boy was so sweet and always smiling. We couldn't help falling in love with him.

Then one day, after a couple of busy months without seeing them, we arrived to find their one-year-old extremely sick and dehydrated. He looked the size of a six-month-old and was so lethargic that he could hardly move his skinny little body. We got him to the hospital as quickly as possible so they could put him on IV. We feared it was too late. But he held on.

One day I walked into the hospital room to find the grandmother feeding the baby a bottle of some sort of vile dark blue concoction. Malak's young wife looked helpless and explained that the grandmother had gone to the *marabou*—the local version of a traditional healer or witchdoctor. His "prescription" was some Qur'anic verses written in ink on a piece of paper and shaken up with unsanitized water in the baby's bottle. The doctors had made no objection.

There have been few times in my adult life that I've really lost my temper. This was one of them. We didn't have a problem accepting local customs, but this one was a matter of life and death. We put out a request to everyone on our prayer list that the Enemy's deception would not succeed in bringing death to this innocent little soul.

Then things got worse. Stephen was at the hospital one day, helping out with some of the medical bills, when suddenly three policemen burst in and arrested Malak on suspicion of being a Christian and being in possession of Christian materials.

Stephen struggled with whether to intervene. He finally recognized that getting himself involved would only make it more difficult for Malak, so we prayed and fasted. I continued to visit the hospital to bring food to the mother and to pray over the sweet baby, hoping to model the love and compassion of Christ. Little by little the child regained some strength, and I was delighted to see him nibbling on the bananas that I brought each day. God was to prove his amazing faithfulness yet again.

Just a few days later, Malak was released from jail, and the day after that, his son was sent home from hospital. We were overjoyed to walk into their home and find the family back together, the baby eating well and almost back to normal size. We prayed that the couple would have the wisdom to keep their little one healthy, and we trusted that the whole experience would only serve to strengthen our friend's faith.

But then it happened. A few weeks later some newspaper articles came out about Malak, Stephen, and our work. The article showed pictures of Bibles and other materials we'd handed out, alleging that we had hired Malak to be an evangelist and that we had already paid one thousand people to become Christians. One paper we read was trying to incite an even bigger problem: "What is the government going to do about these Christians?" it asked. "Is it going to allow them to continue working here until our nation becomes a Christian republic? Or until they go to our ancient cities and are allowed to climb up the ancient mosques?"

This was a mess. A dangerous mess. But God encouraged us through his Word. We were to rest in the Lord and wait patiently for him, not worrying because of human efforts against us (Psalm 37:7; 112:7). We were reminded not to think it strange that a "fiery trial" had come to try us but to rejoice that we were "partakers of Christ's sufferings" (1 Peter 4:12-13, KJV). We were to keep our eyes on the unseen, where this light and temporary affliction was working for us "a far more exceeding and eternal weight of glory" (2 Corinthians 4:17, KJV).

Courageously, Stephen went to the newspaper and met with the journalist and photographer to try and set the story straight. To our surprise, he seemed to get through to them.

They agreed to retract the article. But Malak had people constantly watching him after that—and we soon realized that we weren't out of danger just yet either. A few weeks later, another paper printed an article about Stephen with more "incriminating" pictures of Christian materials and another claim that our NGO was paying locals to become Christians. Again Stephen went to the newspaper's office in person and managed to get an audience with the journalist. Once again his insistence paid off, and the paper retracted its false statements.

We were concerned about the potential backlash all this negative publicity could have on our work at the training center, but thankfully enrollments continued as normal, and the local authorities didn't pressure us in any way. But I couldn't help feeling like we were in a war zone.

Our next scare was close to home. Phoebe and Grace noticed they were being watched each time they were out playing with the kids in the street or visiting the kids' families. One day a car pulled up near Phoebe and the kids she was playing with, and a man began taking photos of them from the window. Stephen took the incident very seriously. We worried about the possibility of another damaging article. Fortunately none appeared, but it had been a close call.

CHAPTER 14

Money Is the Root

"**IF YOU HAVE THE OPPORTUNITY** to steal something, take it—it's an opportunity that God has given you. It's only a sin if you get caught."

A friend of Phoebe's from a very upper-class family explained this to her one day. We had learned that the moral fabric of this society resembled its physical backdrop—individual cracks and bits of rubbish may have seemed small, but together they created a rather devastating and depressive landscape. The daily instances of corruption, dishonesty, greed, and hypocrisy made for one big mess. Dishonesty and "looking out for number one" was simply the way of life.

As wonderful and hospitable as this society was, people's

highest priority was survival. It was socially and religiously acceptable to be deceptive in your personal life, in business, or in government. As in many developing countries, corruption was obvious, and the easiest solution was to turn a blind eye. Beneath the surface of friendly transactions often lay a selfish motive, and we found that it was challenging to try to launch new projects completely "above the table." Everywhere Stephen turned, he was faced with dishonesty and bribery.

· I never really saw Stephen get mad, but I sensed a righteous anger in him. He was committed to maintaining integrity no matter how difficult it was. And as part of that, he felt that he must also expect integrity from others. This certainly set him apart. Although it made our projects more stressful and complicated, Stephen's resolution affected many—from prisoners all the way to the minister of justice. Stephen had won the trust and respect of so many. When he spoke, people listened intently. Government officials appreciated our work and trusted us to do whatever program we thought would benefit the people. Whenever other NGOs requested government approval to do a project in the prison, they were told to go through our NGO because ours was the only one the government trusted. We enjoyed the favor, but we didn't realize how solid this bond of trust would turn out to be.

Throughout our years here, people were attracted to Stephen because of his integrity, and he had ample opportunity to share what had changed his life. But at times it was a little tricky to separate the sheep from the goats, even among the existing believers we got to know along the way. There were a handful of believers who had been led to Christ and discipled by various expats, some of whom had left the country before we arrived. We were always happy to meet a brother or sister, but in some cases, the older believers lacked Christlike character and maturity, and their motives were not always innocent. Many expected more than just spiritual gifts from us "rich foreigners." Some were very blatant in asking for handouts.

"Give us a goat," one asked us before we'd even gotten through the first half of the customary greetings. These new acquaintances—a young couple—had been discipled by some other expats who had recently left the country and who had asked whether we could continue the discipling process.

"We don't have a goat to give," Stephen replied. I sat down beside the young wife and asked how she was doing. She leaned over and mumbled, "Give me a twenty dollars."

It turned out to be an awkward evening. The family was not rich, but they certainly weren't as poor as most of our friends, who asked us for nothing. Stephen tried to explain that we didn't have much to help them with financially but that we were looking forward to their friendship. But the couple had no interest in a friendship—they just wanted money. When we left, we made the decision that we should focus our efforts elsewhere.

The twisted morality drove us crazy—and sometimes it hit very close to home. Our friend Amir, who helped in loan follow-ups and visits with the cooperatives, started taking some of the loan payments to use for other purposes. When Stephen confronted him, Amir said, puzzled, "What's wrong? I just borrowed it. I was going to pay it back." Amir explained that he had to help a friend. The friend knew that he had the money, and it would have brought tremendous shame on him not to lend it. Where the money came from, or where the money actually belonged, was secondary. Amir was clearly feeling justified, and he couldn't understand why Stephen was making a fuss about it. Stephen realized it had been a mistake to mix this relationship with work. He decided to relieve Amir of his job, in hopes of salvaging the friendship and continuing with visits and study sessions together. We could only pray that Amir and our other brothers and sisters would not be conformed to the pattern of *this* world but would be transformed by the renewing of their minds.

But we couldn't have predicted how Satan would attack the local believers in this area in such a profound and devastating way. A well-meaning but ill-informed US organization had decided that the best approach to support the emerging body of believers in closed countries was a grassroots strategy. They planned to send finances directly to indigenous churches and pastors, completely bypassing any expatriate workers on the field, which would cut down on costs and administration. In theory it sounded like a great idea, but it would spell disaster in our country. The local believers were still very immature in their faith, and we knew firsthand their struggles with greed, dishonesty, and other cultural baggage. As soon as we got wind of the organization's intent, Stephen pleaded with them to rethink their plans for this particular country. They wouldn't listen. They assumed that since the strategy had worked so well in India, it should work anywhere.

The word quickly got out that money was going to be sent to various local pastors. Next thing we knew, several men were suddenly "pastors," and only a few of the believers stayed connected to the expats. The benefactors cut ties with the expat group who'd been working with them. They were given a large sum of money to purchase a property on which to build their new "underground church." We knew what was coming. Within days of the well-meaning donor's departure, the new property had been resold and the money distributed among greedy hands.

Stephen decided to confront the locals involved. Sweeping these kinds of issues under the rug had seriously stunted the growth of the church in the past. He tried to handle it biblically, first confronting them individually, then as a group, but they responded in anger and started spreading rumors about Stephen. Dissension spread like cancer, infiltrating even the other expat workers. Other conflict issues on our team had been intensifying for the past year, and Stephen didn't have the support he needed from all of his own coworkers. But whatever the cost, Stephen was not prepared to back down on what was right, even he knew he was treading on a field of land mines.

It wasn't long before one exploded. A series of articles appeared on the web, divulging sensitive information about Stephen and all the workers connected to us, describing the work we were doing, what cars we drove, and where we lived. No specific names were mentioned, but it was hardly necessary.

Stephen and the few believers trying to defend him had a pretty strong hunch who'd written the articles. It seemed to be an obvious case of revenge, as the articles expounded particularly on Stephen. This particular website was a haven for Islamic fundamentalists—and they would easily recognize who the articles were about. They knew who Stephen was.

CHAPTER 15

Restless

STEPHEN HAD RETURNED home one evening looking a little distracted. He'd received a strange phone call that afternoon while out playing ball with Joshua. He didn't go into any detail but told me not to worry too much about it. But over the next day or two, he seemed a little more cautious than usual. One morning after he left to take Piper to school, he called to ask whether there was still a red car parked out in front of our house. There wasn't, but as I thought about it, I had noticed a strange red car parking across the road now and then.

But it could mean anything. Or nothing.

On a Thursday evening when Stephen came home, he

seemed uncharacteristically restless. Normally he would grab five or ten minutes to lie down to take a breather and read his devotional, but this evening he had his *Daily Light* devotional under his nose while he paced back and forth slowly across the room. He seemed engulfed by what he was reading.

As he visited with a local seeker and another North African brother that night, I felt such a presence of the Lord in the room that I lingered outside the door, trying to hear what was being said. Eventually I gave up, and after I served them the third cup of tea, I went to bed.

The visit went very late that night, and Stephen was a bit late getting Piper off to school the next morning. In all our years of marriage, he would never leave the house without grabbing a hug, but this particular morning we were in such a tizzy that he almost rushed out without one.

Just as he was about to walk out the door he stopped and turned around. "What, no hug this morning?"

I stopped what I was doing and smiled. "Sorry!" I gave him an extra-long hug to make up for almost missing him. Then off he went.

I went on with my morning, getting Joshua up to start his schoolwork. I was sitting at the table with him, poring over his science books, when we were interrupted by a frantic knock at the door. Laura, one of our teammates, stood at the threshold, completely distraught.

The only time I'd ever seen Laura cry in the whole seven years we'd known her was when her son had become extremely ill and they thought they were going to lose him.

Something was terrible must have happened. "What's wrong? What's wrong?" I started asking urgently.

But before saying a word she gently ushered me back into the house. We went into one of the rooms and I closed the door. She took my arm and sat us both down. With her voice trembling, she finally said the words.

"Something terrible has happened . . ." She took a shuddering breath and forced herself to make eye contact. "Stephen has been shot."

A million scenarios flashed through my mind. I knew *her* husband, also named Stephen, had been traveling in the interior—what had happened? I began trying to console her. But she shook her head.

"No, not my Stephen," she said slowly. The pain in her eyes cut me to the core. "Your Stephen was shot. He's dead."

CHAPTER 16

Then Came the Rain

I FELT AS IF MY HEART had stopped beating. A few eternal seconds passed. Then it began pounding so hard I couldn't breathe, and I was sure my chest was going to explode.

The words floated around my ears, vainly attempting to penetrate my skull. I just stared at Laura in disbelief. Surely she was wrong. Surely I was dreaming. Surely it was a cruel mistake. He couldn't be dead. Maybe he *was* shot, but only injured. Or they only thought it was Stephen, but it was probably someone else. *No! No! No! This is not happening!*

But I couldn't fully deny it. I had to pull myself together. My mind was racing, running ahead. *How am I going to tell my kids? How am I going to tell Stephen's parents?*

I resisted the emotions boiling inside me. I pushed back the urge to scream and cry—to run away.

Then the shock kicked in. My mind clicked over into survival mode. *Are they still on the loose—the men who killed Stephen? Could they be coming here? Do we need to get out of here? What should we do?*

"We need to get you and the kids out of here," Laura said, as though reading my mind. "The men who shot Stephen got away. You need to come with me to my house."

Everyone in this city knows Stephen and where we live. My mind felt miraculously clear. I knew what we had to do. I brought the older three children into the room and sat them down in front of me. They knew right away that something was wrong. I looked at them and forced myself to say the words.

"Something terrible has happened to your dad . . ."

"Is he okay?" Heidi was not at all satisfied with the information.

I felt as if I were choking on the words as they came out. "No . . . he's not." That was all I could bring myself to say. For now, my mind would not accept what I'd been told. I clung to some desperate hope that Laura was wrong. Maybe he'd been shot, but he was still alive.

I got each of the kids to find a small bag, and we began packing for the unknown. I grabbed some money, our passports, and a change of clothes. Within ten minutes we were in Laura's car, driving to the other side of town.

The route took us around the outskirts of the city. I sat

in the passenger seat, staring out the window. On one side I could see the ocean of buildings in this city we'd fallen in love with . . . on the other, the endless desert dunes. There was complete silence in the car. I finally let a tiny bit of reality creep its way in, terrifying as it was. I realized I hadn't shed a tear or even prayed yet. I longed to cry out to the Lord, but what would I say? Bless him? Curse him for allowing this to happen?

Finally, I cried out in my heart the only words that made sense, the only thing I could draw up from the sorrow threatening to overwhelm me. *You have to be glorified, God! You have to be glorified! Please tell me you are glorified. If you are glorified, then I'll know this was not all in vain. Because I know he was willing to give his life and I know you are worthy!*

I felt a gentle wind blow through my spirit. *I AM glorified today.*

It is a miraculous thing to hear the voice of God. And in that moment, at the sound of his voice, I felt a deep and indescribable peace. In the midst of a whirlwind of conflicting emotions, I knew that the love of my life was fully satisfied in the presence of the One he so deeply loved and so selflessly served. I felt a gaping hole in my heart as the reality of my loss sunk in, but somehow beneath that void, I was content. Quiet. Calm. Simply because the only One who meant even more to me than Stephen was . . . glorified. I would never be tempted to ask why—though I may never really understand the why in this life.

When we got to Laura's house, I knew I had to talk to

the kids. Piper was still at school and hadn't heard the news yet, so a friend who carpooled with us would go and pick up her daughter and Piper, who were best friends. I was facing the most heart-wrenching and difficult thing I've ever had to do in my life—I needed to share the depth of the news with each of my children. I started with Heidi. I took her into a room, closed the door, and sat her down beside me. I felt so at a loss for words. So helpless. "I'm so sorry, Heidi. Your dad was shot this morning, and he has gone to be with Jesus." She broke down immediately, and I sat and hugged her as she cried. My heart ached.

"We'll get through this," I told her after she'd had a few minutes for it to sink in. "God will help us through it."

She looked up at me with an unusual courage in her eyes. "I know. It's okay." She'd begun wiping away the tears and pulling herself together. I could tell she was being strong for her siblings and me. She had always been so mature for her age. I wanted so badly to shelter her and the others from the pain of their loss.

Next I told twelve-year-old Ellie, and I held her as she wept. My heart broke as I prayed over her. She had such a tender spirit. Her daddy's nickname for her was "Sweet Ellie." I prayed that she would forever remember the wonderful relationship they'd had.

Then it was Joshua's turn. I found him sitting in one of the rooms with the door closed, clearly already in shock. As I told him, I could see he was trying his best not to cry. He didn't say anything, so I sat there just to be with him for a while. I prayed for God's grace to fill his heart, knowing he was battling too many emotions to make sense of. He was so brave. As I sat and prayed over him, I sensed a warfare beginning in the heavenlies over my son's soul and his calling. I didn't quite understand it at the moment, but I found myself waging war against the Enemy in his life, a war I would be fighting for all of my kids over the coming years.

"Do you just want some time alone?" I asked him after a few minutes.

"Yeah."

He didn't come out for a long time. Later in the day, he put on a brave, smiling face as he spoke to our visitors. "My dad's a hero." I could see that he was still in shock and it hadn't really hit him yet, but he wanted to be brave and make the best of the situation, just as his dad would have done.

Finally I sat down with my little seven-year-old Piper. When I told her what had happened, she immediately just wanted to run off and play, as if she refused to give any thought to what I was saying. Denial was clearly the only way she could cope right now. She went off and started playing with her friend as if nothing had happened.

Who knew how a seven-year-old brain could deal with this kind of information? My adult brain couldn't even begin to comprehend it.

I could hardly face the call to Stephen's parents, but I knew it had to be done. With the five-hour time difference, they'd still be asleep when it happened, but by 5:30 a.m. Eastern Time I couldn't put it off any longer. Still I just couldn't face telling them over the phone—it just didn't seem fair for them to hear it that way. I decided to call Stephen's brother instead and then ask him to relay the news in person. Next I called my parents. It was painful for us to be so far away from our family during this crisis. The miles between us had always been hard, but today it felt as though they were in another galaxy. As difficult as it was for us, it was torturing them not to be able to be with us.

Laura was trying her best to help with the kids and make us comfortable. "The embassy just called," she informed me quietly. "They are sending over a couple of people to talk to you about what steps need to be made to get you the belongings Stephen had with him and also help make arrangements to get you and the children and Stephen's remains to the US." I felt a sharp pain shoot through my numb heart at the words "Stephen's remains."

Within an hour there was a knock at the door. I felt a wave of dread wash over me at the very thought of having to process this with anyone from the embassy. I sat there on the chair, holding a full glass of water that Laura had been trying to get me to drink. As Laura opened the door, I heard the voices of two Arab men.

The director of human rights and the minister of justice were ushered into the room where I sat. How these men had found out where we were so quickly was a mystery. The fact that they arrived even before the embassy personnel proved to me how badly they wanted to see us.

"*Salaam alaykum*, Madam Foreman," the minister of

justice said. "We have come to pay our most sincere condolences." His head hung low, and his voice was shaking as he spoke.

"Thank you," I said with as much courtesy as I could muster. Then there was an awkward silence for several minutes. I was taken aback when I noticed one of them wiping tears from his eyes. Was he really crying? Muslim men in this culture didn't cry, especially in public! For any Muslim to cry in public over a loss like this would be to insult Allah and his will.

"Your husband was a good man. A godly man," said the director. "We all loved him."

"Yes, and we cannot believe that the men who killed your husband are from this country," said the minister of justice. "If they are indeed from this country, then they could not have possibly known him. If they had known your husband, they could have never harmed him. Rest assured, Madam Foreman, we will not rest until these dogs are brought to justice. We beg you, please continue the work that your husband began here. Please don't allow his legacy to die as well."

They said their kind words of peace and blessing over our family, and then they were gone. I was deeply touched by their sincere words, though I couldn't process the significance of that visit at that moment. It would be several days before I would realize and appreciate the respect and favor that God had given Stephen and our family in this country.

Finally the workers from the US embassy arrived, asking questions and explaining the investigation process and other legalities. I would need to accompany them to the police station to collect Stephen's belongings that afternoon.

Meanwhile, word had gotten around the city faster than a sandstorm. The people began pouring in, mostly workers and expats, all coming to be with us and offer their support. Our location was kept secret from the locals for our security. But somehow a friend whom I didn't see often and who worked with the fire department managed to track me down. She vowed to me that they were going to find the perpetrators.

The regional security officer of the US embassy told me that the road to our own house was completely swamped with people wanting to come and pay their condolences and be with our family. "Mrs. Foreman, it is not safe for you to return to your home right now," he cautioned. "Locals are lined up all the way down the street and are refusing to go home until they see you."

The embassy strongly advised that I not go back to the house during the day because the culprits hadn't yet been caught and they had no way of knowing who was who. I was inexplicably unafraid. I wanted with all of my heart to go be with my local friends and family. If it cost my life, so be it. My life meant nothing to me now. But only because my kids meant everything to me, I complied.

I was still numb with shock. All this time I had shed very few tears. I'd never been one to cry in public. Growing up, if I were ever feeling hurt, I'd wait to be alone with my pillow to cry it out. I felt compelled to hold it together for my kids' sake, and I knew there were important matters at hand I'd have to deal with.

Soon my phone started ringing nonstop. All of my friends had heard the news, and everybody wanted to speak to me. I couldn't bring myself to answer their calls.

No one had asked me whether I wanted to go see Stephen's body, and perhaps I wouldn't even have been able to for security reasons. *Do I want to go? Do I need that for closure?* What a decision to make. It would take a long time for me to come to terms with the fact that he'd actually been shot in the face. I only wanted to remember him the way I'd last seen him as I'd hugged him good-bye that morning: his gorgeous brown eyes smiling down at me and his strong, warm arms wrapped around me. I was petrified that what I would see now would erase my last memory. *No! I won't let that go!* my spirit screamed in protest. Finally, I decided I couldn't go. A kind friend offered to escort his body to the hospital morgue.

When the embassy escorted me to our appointment at the police station, we arrived to a huge crowd of people. The first faces I saw were our adoptive local family, Ali's family. They'd already been to our house and had tried everything to get in touch with me. I longed for that connection but wasn't able to stop and talk with them as the embassy workers ushered me into the station.

Ali was at least allowed in to help us translate. He looked very pale. He was clearly devastated and in shock, but he was clearheaded nonetheless. After some waiting we were finally taken into a back room where Stephen's things were splayed out on a desk. The police had gone through all the contents, which included some Bibles, tracts, and several JESUS films. I took a seat as the herd of police staff began making notes of all the contents. In the end the embassy people got so frustrated with the whole process that they insisted the police hand over all the contents and allow me to go. To our relief the police agreed.

As we came out of the building, the security guards were holding everyone back, but I could see Ali's family still waiting for me. I broke away from my escorts and ran over to hug my sisters. I had been to funerals with them and had never seen them crying outright. But this day, they wept. Somehow, seeing this uncharacteristic show of emotion gave me special comfort. It gave proof of their deep love for Stephen and our family. They were grieving with me. I hoped in my heart that through our deep relationship with their family they were coming to a new understanding of Allah. We said our farewells, not knowing when we'd see each other again. They were some of the only friends I was able to say good-bye to.

The rest of the day was a blur. The shock had long set in like a concrete mold, crushing and numbing me. There were things I needed to get from the house . . . plane tickets to organize for me and the kids . . . and Stephen's body.

The embassy workers would be picking me up soon to go and speak to the airline. As I sat waiting, I could feel the block of shock slowly starting to crumble. My arms and legs started hurting badly, probably from the stress of my heart beating so hard for such a long time. All at once I felt completely exhausted. Everything seemed to be happening behind a hazy screen. I tried to receive the next batch of expat friends coming to pay their condolences, but all I craved was solitude. I was thankful when the embassy people called to say our meeting with airline would be the next morning.

The kids were bedded down on mats around me. Amazingly, in a strange house, in strange beds, with no air-conditioning, after the day we'd had, they'd somehow gone to sleep. My mind replayed the conversation I had had with each of them earlier that day, and I marveled at God's grace. I felt I understood the true depth of Philippians 4:7: "And the peace of God, which transcends all understanding, will guard your hearts and your minds in Christ Jesus."

"Oh God, please guard their little hearts and minds," I begged. I knew that the Enemy would like nothing more than attack our hearts and minds with this tragedy.

I lay in bed for a good hour or so, boring holes into the ceiling with my eyes. The reality of my loss began to sink in. I felt as though half my body had been amputated. I lay there wishing so hard that I could wake up from this horrific nightmare.

I still hadn't really cried. I couldn't allow myself to lose control.

Suddenly, a light flashed through the window. *Somebody's trying to look in with a flashlight,* I thought, panicked. *Surely they couldn't have found us!* But when I got up and looked out into the darkness, there wasn't a soul in sight.

Another sudden flash lit up the sky. Lightning. I was amazed. Thunderstorms were so rare in the desert, let alone in June. I lay back down on the bed. A thunderclap sounded in the distance, and with that clap, something started to break inside me.

The next moment, a steady rain began to fall. As I listened to the gentle drumming, I heard a quiet voice whisper, *I'm grieving with you.*

That was all it took. The dam broke. Soon my pillow was as soaked as the sodden ground outside.

And the rain kept falling.

I'm here. I'm grieving with you . . .

At that same hour, a lone man stood on an empty street.

Amir had heard about the shooting that afternoon but didn't want to believe it. He'd driven straight to the site to see for himself, but it had been blocked off for miles and he couldn't even get close. Finally he'd given up and gone home, determined to return after dark. It had been easy enough to find. The blood still marked the spot.

He stood there now, staring at the blood-drenched sand, tears running down his face.

Slowly he lifted his face to the sky. "Why this man, Lord?" he cried. "Why him? He was such a good man! What are we, your followers, going to do now that he's gone?"

Suddenly, lightning flashed, illuminating the wine-red scar.

And then came the rain.

He watched as the water began to wash the blood into the soil. Then he heard a still, small voice.

Look, Amir. I'm watering the seed that has fallen. But it will multiply.

A new strength came over Amir. A courage unlike anything he'd ever experienced.

"God, if you are worthy of my brother Stephen's life, then you are surely worthy of mine!"

CHAPTER 17

Fog

I WOKE BEFORE DAWN the next morning with a sense of numbness. I walked into the dimly lit kitchen, where Laura was already making tea. She looked up at me with hollow eyes. "You need to drink something, Emily," she said. "You will dehydrate before you know it." I had always admired Laura's strength. She brought a sense of stability to the situation, and her nursing skills were often to our advantage. I was thankful to have her with me now. I sat down and forced down a cup of water. I didn't want to eat or drink. I just wanted to wake up from this nightmare.

"The embassy called to inform us that the men are still on the loose," Laura told me. Her words sounded very far away. "They don't want you to leave this house without the regional security officer escorting you. He is coming in a couple of hours to take you to the embassy to help you get tickets and leave as soon as possible."

Leave as soon as possible? I can't leave! I don't want to leave! I can't leave the country where Stephen's life just ended! My mind and my heart were screaming. I tried so hard to make sense of it, but I couldn't. It felt as though to leave this place was to leave Stephen's life behind.

I sat quietly as the embassy worker searched for tickets on her computer and waited impatiently on hold with Delta. The flights were all full, but with much persuasion, the director of Delta managed to bump a few people to squeeze us in on the flight leaving the following day.

Then we got to the even more dreaded subject of the repatriation of Stephen's body. My heart sank. I couldn't bear the thought. Despite the kindness and sensitivity of the embassy workers, my heart began to race again, and I felt incredibly weak. As my sense of helplessness intensified, my mind drifted back to my kids. My poor kids.

The next morning, we stealthily returned to our house at 4:00 a.m. before the first call to prayer. Security guards were guarding the house and the road. We began packing up our most important belongings with the help of our expat friends. I couldn't imagine having to do this without them. After I'd packed the last of my things, I went to the basket of dirty clothes in the bathroom and picked up the shirt Stephen had worn the day before his death. Losing the battle with an onslaught of tears, I buried my face in it for a long time, trying to memorize the scent. I breathed in deeply several times, finding myself lost in the sensation that he was still there. My heart ached. This was the last time I'd ever be able to smell him.

For my kids' sakes, I meagerly attempted to regain my composure. The biggest challenge to that attempt came when I went to check on each of them. I watched in agony as they sorted through their belongings, packing the things that were dearest to them. I wondered what was going through their minds. Perhaps it was by the grace of God that they didn't understand the finality of what was going on. Despite the pain I knew each of them was experiencing and the pain we were experiencing together, an air of calm surrounded them, as if they were protected by a bubble of peace—not a peace that the world gives, but divine peace. Peace unexplainable.

We had been unjustifiably robbed of husband and father, but we were not abandoned.

Feeling like burglars, we hauled our luggage out and loaded them in the vehicles. And we left our house and our Neem trees for the last time.

Fatu had been traveling in the southern part of the country and didn't hear the news until two hours before we were due to fly out. The report on her taxi radio didn't mention Stephen's name but described the area and an American man, so she panicked and had the taxi take her straight to the training center, where the worst was confirmed.

When she arrived to see me, she was a complete mess. She

could hardly hold herself together or even walk. Her mother and sisters, who'd come with her, were trying to console her and calm her down—for them, it was shameful that she was showing such emotion. We sat on the floor of my room, neither of us knowing what to say or do. She just sobbed. I felt bad that I wasn't crying with her. My shock blanket had closed in again, and the tears wouldn't come. I was just grateful she was there.

Leaving that day was one of the most difficult things I've ever had to do. There were so many friends I hadn't been able to see, and it hurt me to leave them without so much as a good-bye. Several expat friends accompanied us to the airport. We were greeted by the director of human rights, who had kindly come to see us off. I was touched that he had come, but I wasn't in the mood for company. I just wanted to be somewhere in solitude with my kids so we could process and grieve together.

I sat staring through all the wonderful people who had come to be a support for us, their conversations mingling into a soundless drone, as I tried vainly once again to fathom what had happened and process the fact that I was actually leaving my home. I felt on the verge of a major meltdown at that point, but I was determined to hold it together because we were about to get on the plane. The boarding call finally came—not a moment too soon.

The director of human rights broke all cultural norms by taking my arm to escort me out to the plane. He leaned in close so I would hear him above the roar of the engines.

"Please don't worry. We will not rest until these men are brought to justice. Your family is our family." He promised to keep me informed of the investigation and then handed me his business card with his cell phone number written on the back, insisting that I contact him if he could be of any assistance at all. I thanked him for all his kindness, and we got on the plane. It would take time for these kinds of responses to truly sink in. In the years since, I've begun to really understand the weight of actions such as these. I knew that Stephen—through our projects and through his love for God, his family, and the people of the country—had gained quite an honorable reputation in the city where we lived. He didn't live out his faith privately; he walked out his faith publicly. But I hadn't realized just how profound his impact had been on the lives people there. He left a mark that would not soon be forgotten. And as we sat on the runway getting ready to take off, I felt a deep conviction in my heart that God was not done yet.

The flight to Paris passed in a few numb, colorless hours. Our layover in Paris was a blur as we sat in silence watching news on TV. It all seemed so unimportant. So trivial in comparison to what we were going through. We boarded our next plane and settled in for the long haul. To my relief, Phoebe had offered to travel back with us. She was a stronghold for me as she helped console and entertain the kids.

As we sat on our flight back to the US, I stared out the window, leaning my head against the cold, dark glass. Beyond, it was only black. Cold and black. I couldn't get my mind off the fact that Stephen's body was in a casket in the cargo hold of the plane, instead of having him sitting next to me on the seat.

I opened my bag, remembering an envelope someone had handed me as we were leaving. The elders of the expat Protestant church had written heartfelt words of condolence and consolation. They felt the Lord wanted them to share Psalm 116 with me. I took out my Bible to read it. I had read and contemplated this chapter before, but today it had a deeper meaning.

"Return to your rest, my soul, for the LORD has been good to you. . . . Precious in the sight of the LORD is the death of his faithful servants" (verses 7, 15).

I struggled to maintain my composure. I read it again. And again.

Return to your rest, I would keep reminding myself as anxious thoughts crept in.

Stephen's death is precious to God.

CHAPTER 18

Loss and Found

I BRACED MYSELF AS we landed in Raleigh. The embassy had warned us there could be media attention when we got off the plane, and we'd decided it was best to avoid that until the family was ready to make a full public statement. Fortunately, no journalists galloped toward us with cameramen in tow as we entered the terminal.

To be honest, I was much more anxious about seeing my in-laws. I wanted to be strong for them. I ached for them and the deep loss they, too, were experiencing. I felt like the walking dead and knew that I must have looked it, too. As we neared the final exit gate, my pace slowed. I didn't know how I was going to handle this. I didn't want to face them. But it was unavoidable. I forced my feet to keep walking.

All of Stephen's family and mine were waiting for us. As soon as we caught sight of each other, the barrier was breached. Literally. They plowed past the security barriers and we ran to meet each other. I was blanketed in my parents' embrace for some long minutes. As I finally embraced Stephen's parents, their tears flowing freely, I had to muster every ounce of strength not to dissolve on the spot. I was so tired.

First Baptist Church had kindly loaned the family one of their nice big buses. During the hour-and-a-half drive home, hardly anyone said a word. Stephen's parents were doing their best to maintain their composure for the kids' sake. I was glad to be sitting beside my brother. He wasn't an overtly emotional person, and I felt as if I could sit next to him without falling apart. When we got to my in-laws' house, the kids and I went straight to bed. But even though I'd slept only about four hours in the past three days, sleep would not come. Once again I lay in an empty bed, staring at the pictures on the wall of a youthful and vibrant Stephen. *How could he be gone?*

Over the next three days leading up to the funeral, I had to try and snap myself into some form of semifunctional decision-making mode. First on the agenda was preparing a clear public statement before any misconstrued stories or rumors got out about what we'd been doing in North Africa. We needed to protect our coworkers in the country and the work that we hoped would continue. We were blessed to have a wonderful family friend who was in the police department, and he became our media liaison for all the local news stations and newspapers. He even organized a security guard for my in-laws' house, where we were staying; the criminals were still on the loose, and we weren't ignorant of the fact that terrorists have networks in every Western country.

I was very grateful that my father-in-law had amazing clarity of mind through all the decision making. There were a hundred things to decide and organize for the funeral. Right away we had to pick out a casket and make arrangements at the funeral home. I'd remembered a conversation Stephen and I had had on one of our rare date nights in Africa, only months before his death. "If something happens to me, just bury me here," he'd said out of the blue. He wasn't being sentimental, I realized. He simply wanted to save us the trouble and cost of having his body repatriated. Not only had he been prepared to die, he'd thought even beyond it to matters of our "convenience." As it turned out, our insurance company, a Christian medical group, had not only covered the repatriation but went beyond their obligations and paid for my ticket home as well.

Picking out a casket and other things for the service was surreal. I couldn't bring myself to even process what I "wanted." I only wanted not to be there, doing this. That was all. In light of what I'd just lost, casket designs and flower arrangements held no consequence. Nonetheless, the necessary choices were made. We'd decided to have the visitation and funeral at Stephen's home church rather than the funeral home in case there were more people than the funeral home could accommodate. We couldn't have been prepared for just how many did come.

On Monday evening we had visitation. Standing in front of a closed casket, we stood for five hours as over a thousand people poured down the church aisle to pay their respects. The overwhelming outpouring of love astounded me. People had flown and driven in from all over the place. I knew Stephen had lived an amazing life and impacted a lot of people, but none of us had any idea just how immense that impact had been. Person after person came down the line, completely broken up over the situation, introducing themselves and sharing with us how Stephen had touched their lives. The mayor of the city came. The news stations and newspapers sent journalists to the event, and my father-in-law kindly took the responsibility to offer a statement on behalf of our entire family:

> While his murderers were able to stop Stephen's earthly heartbeat, they could not and were not able to kill his spirit, which belongs to Christ and is now in heaven. Our greatest desire is that Stephen will not have died in vain, and the name of the Lord Jesus Christ will be lifted up through this horrible tragedy. Just as God sent his Son to die for others, our son's life is not too high a price to pay if others come to know Jesus as their Savior as a result of Stephen's untimely death.

David Smith, Stephen's lifelong best friend, also gave a statement:

> One of his goals in life was to be able to say this:
> "For I am already being poured out like a drink
> offering, and the time has come for my departure.
> I have fought the good fight, I have finished the
> race, I have kept the faith. Now there is in store for
> me the crown of righteousness, which the Lord, the
> righteous Judge, will award to me on that day—
> and not only to me, but all who have longed for
> his appearing" (2 Timothy 4:6-8). His life was not
> taken; he gave his life.

At the funeral the following day, cars lined the street for miles in both directions as people arrived in droves. I felt as if I were in a dream the entire day. As our procession drove to the gravesite afterward, it seemed that every person in town knew exactly what was going on and whom this was for. On every street we drove down, people came out and stood with their hats on their hearts or stopped their cars in reverence.

I was completely unaware of everyone around me. I had no idea who had come to the gravesite. I wouldn't realize what a crowd filled the cemetery until we looked at photos afterward. It was a beautiful day as the sun beamed down from an azure sky, dappling the lush grass beneath spreading cedar trees. I was deeply thankful for Stephen's brother, who had found an ideal burial site that lay in a historical section, at the convergence of a military graveyard, a slave graveyard, and a peasant graveyard—only fitting for a man who was always a friend to all.

At first, moving back to the States had created for us somewhat of an alternate universe. This otherworldly state of mind, doubly blanketed in the shroud of shock and busyness, had shielded the kids and me and made it easier for us to cope, at least on a surface level. But after the funeral, reality finally started sinking its teeth in. I felt utterly run down, exhausted, and overcome.

At last, I slept. But the momentary oblivion almost wasn't worth the black cloud that descended with fresh, suffocating force upon each awakening. My mind and body would have preferred to hibernate for a good few weeks, but I felt that we should stay on with my in-laws for a while. The house was being flooded with visitors, and I felt obliged to show my face, drawn and pale as it was. I piled on the makeup as best I could to cover the dark crescents under my eyes. I didn't mind the visits, though. I loved the people who came, and their kindness—the cards, the flowers, the meals cooked with love—touched me afresh with each knock on the door. The flood of love buoyed us all up above sinking level, and God's presence was tangible in the house. For weeks on end, the cards and letters kept pouring in from all over the country and other corners of the globe—condolences, encouragement, and testimony after testimony of how God had inspired hearts and lives through Stephen's story. Many came from people who had never heard Stephen's name before it appeared in the news. We were truly astounded and uplifted to see God glorified in so many ways through both Stephen's life and death. That had always been Stephen's goal.

A memorial service was held in Texas a few weeks later. Many people came from the various churches all over Texas with which we'd had relationships, along with students, staff, and alumni from the ministry schools on campus. It was a challenging experience being there, with so many memories and sympathetic faces to wrench my heart and push my composure to the limit.

The hardest part came when the event organizers sat me down to give me a chance to preview the video tribute to Stephen. It was the first time I'd seen footage of him since his death, and it was all I could do to hold myself together. That evening I took the DVD back to my room. I must have played it over a hundred times.

I'd been asked whether I'd like to speak at the service, but I didn't have the strength for it. The real magnitude of my loss was starting to dawn on me.

Just before we left for the memorial service in Texas, dear friends who had been an encouragement to our family and supporters of our work over the years offered the kids and me a wonderful little house to live in. The house was situated in the countryside, surrounded by greenery and solitude. I was so blessed by their offer, and I couldn't think of anywhere else more suitable. *This is only temporary,* I told myself. *We'll be going back home.*

As the nights passed, my loss became more painfully real. The various aspects of grief came in monstrous waves. I would just be coming up for air when another would crash over me, sending me tumbling back into grief's dreaded grip. In the beginning I was feeling the loss of my in-laws' son and my children's father. Then I had to face the all-consuming loss of my husband and best friend. Almost daily I would look out the window of the kitchen and fantasize that Stephen would be walking up the driveway, smiling and saying, "It's okay. It was only a dream." Finally, the loss of our home and friends in North Africa broke over me with fresh force. It would take me many months to start feeling anywhere in the outer realm of "normal."

All through the stormy ocean, my Savior was in my boat even in the times I felt he was sleeping. I also began to understand more of the intimacy of his role as my Shepherd. I was walking through the valley, but my Shepherd showed me that the shadow of death that tempted me to feel hopeless and defeated was only a shadow. Besides the many wonderful and helpful books people gave me, the Scriptures remained my anchor through the storm. I had the same *Daily Light* devotional that Stephen used to read, and the Holy Spirit never failed to bring me a word in season through its pages.

I certainly had my nights, though. The grief always seemed to hit worst when the distractions of the day with four busy kids had ceased. As I would finally exhale and get myself ready for bed, the silence would creep up on me, and the magnitude of my loneliness would settle over me like a dank, heavy blanket. One night it weighed me down so heavily that I resorted to taking medicine to fall asleep. But I still woke up in the middle of the night, overcome by sorrow and aloneness.

I felt like I was the last person on earth.

I sobbed for way too long, until my head throbbed and I could hardly see out of my swollen eyes. I knew God's presence was there, but I couldn't really figure out what was different this time. Usually I wouldn't ask people to join my pity parties—I only invited God— but this particular night I felt that I needed someone to pray for me. I knew I could call any given person at two or three in the morning and they would be on their knees in an instant, but somehow I just couldn't bring myself to do it. I lay there for a long time, getting more and more uncomfortable as pain hammered my skull. At last I sat up. I noticed my *Daily Light* on the nightstand. Then it occurred to me that I hadn't read the devotional for the day. I went into the living room and turned on a lamp and huddled into an armchair. With what little vision I had left, I started reading. The Scripture was from John 17, where Jesus was praying for his disciples during his last moments with them before his betrayal:

I pray for them. I am not praying for the world, but for those you have given me, for they are yours. . . .

My prayer is not that you take them out of
the world but that you protect them from the evil
one. . . .
My prayer is not for them alone. I pray also for
those who will believe in me through their message.
(17:9, 15, 20)

Look, the Lord whispered, *I'm praying for you.*

I noticed that when he prayed for his disciples and for me,
he didn't ask God to protect me from harm and suffering. He
went much deeper and prayed that God would protect me
from the Evil One, who would want nothing more than to
fill my heart with bitterness against my God.

I wept even more, a weeping that seemed to cleanse my
heart of any seed of bitterness or depression. I needed prayer.
And my Savior prayed.

"You know," I confessed to the kids, "I cry very hard in the
shower most times, and I usually cry myself to sleep."

While the kids didn't see me fall apart too often in public,
I didn't want them to think I wasn't dealing with it. I prayed
so hard for the wisdom to help them through the grieving
process, and I felt the Lord encouraging me to just be open
with them and invite them to do the same. It was unbearably
hard. But my being honest during the most difficult times
helped them to start opening up to me, and they told me
it was pretty much the same for them. We were never the

perfect family, but we had an unbreakable bond between us, and from that we all drew comfort.

Within a few weeks of Stephen's death, we received the news that the police had arrested the murder suspects following a shoot-out with some Islamist militants in the same area where they had killed Stephen. When I finally stopped to think about the perpetrators, I had mixed feelings. Of course I felt angry, confused, and frustrated, but I didn't want revenge. I couldn't stop thinking, *If they could only realize whom they had killed. They would be sorry! If they could just see a picture of him with his kids . . . would they not realize what they'd done?* I felt as if that conviction alone would surely be punishment enough. I could only remind myself what Stephen had always said: *They were captives, held hostage in their minds. In their deception, they must have honestly believed they were doing the right thing.*

Then on other days I would think that perhaps it had nothing to do with religion—maybe it was all about greed and getting a big payoff. God only knows. But by God's grace I found the capacity to forgive them. My heart broke more and more for them as time went on. One day I got the picture off the Web of the guy who'd pulled the trigger, and my heart sank. He couldn't have been much over twenty. He would have still had his whole life ahead of him. I started praying for him, for all of them. Even as I prayed for them a deep hatred began to well up within my heart. Not a hatred of the sinners, but the sin. A hatred for the deception of the Enemy. Yes, I longed for justice, but somehow it was balanced by the longing for grace. One of the greatest mysteries of our sovereign God is that justice and grace coexist in his character.

The topic of forgiveness was one I hadn't yet broached directly with the kids. Although Piper expressed her grief most openly, I sensed she was having the hardest time processing the whole issue in her mind. One day I came out of the grocery store to find Piper hysterical in the car. She was already tired after a rough day at school, and Joshua had been picking at her, as older brothers do. But it was obvious that she was upset about something more than just her annoying big brother. I got her out of the car to talk to her.

"What's really wrong, honey?" I asked as I began trying to console her.

After a few moments she confessed, "Mommy, I've been praying and asking God for permission to hate those men who killed my daddy."

I was blown away that on her own she had already processed that she should forgive and that she felt she should at least ask God's permission to be bitter instead. It opened the door for us to talk and pray it through together.

From then on, I would bring the topic up in devotions once in a while to see how everyone was doing. Sweet-tempered little Ellie admitted that she'd been confused at first, but she knew God had a reason for everything, and she'd decided to forgive those men because God forgave her. Heidi and Joshua dialogued more with each other than with me. I sensed Joshua was having a harder time with it, but I knew God would work in his heart in his own time.

The question of *why* that many people are left asking after a pointless or accidental death never haunted us in our processing journey because there was one thing none of us ever doubted: Stephen's life had not been stolen from him or from us. Like James Calvert, missionary to the cannibals of Fiji, Stephen had lived by these words: "We died before we came here." Stephen had handed over his life a long time ago. No bullet could have taken it from him. He had willingly given it so that more of his brothers and sisters could join him in worship on the other side of eternity, where the Father's comforting hand and proud smile would wipe away every trace of pain and sorrow.

This reward was worth any price, and the price had not been paid in vain. God confirmed it to all of us over and over in the weeks and months that followed. No, we couldn't see the bigger picture yet. But we knew God saw it, and that was enough.

Though Stephen didn't go out looking to die a martyr, he had always known he might very well be one of the "number" mentioned in Revelation. God had cultivated his heart early on, and he was ready. Even the night before his death, God had somehow prepared him for what was to come.

I couldn't shake the memory of how, the night before he died, Stephen had paced back and forth in our bedroom, poring over Scriptures in his devotional. What I discovered when I looked up what he was reading convinced me more than ever that God's Word is still alive, and he still uses it to speak truth, life, comfort, and grace.

See how he loved (John 11:36).

He died for all. (2 Corinthians 5:15).

Greater love has no one than this: to lay down one's life for one's friends. (John 15:13).

He . . . lives to make intercession for them. (Hebrews 7:25, NASB).

I go to prepare a place for you. . . . I will come again and receive you to Myself, that where I am, there you may be also. (John 14:2-3, NASB).

Father, I desire that they also, whom You have given Me, be with Me where I am (John 17:24, NASB).

Having loved His own who were in the world, He loved them to the end (John 13:1, NASB).

We love him, because he first loved us (1 John 4:19, KJV).

The love of Christ compels us, because we judge thus; that if One died for all, then all died; and He died for all, that those who live should live no longer for themselves, but for Him who died for them and rose again (2 Corinthians 5:14-15, NKJV).

If you keep My commandments, you will abide in My love, just as I have kept My Father's commandments and abide in His love (John 15:10, NKJV).

In his Word, Jesus promises that whoever loses his or her life for Jesus' sake will find it. And yes, in this life I have lost. I lost my husband and best friend. My children lost their father. But I take great comfort in knowing that Stephen didn't lose his life.

He found it.

The Rain Continues

ALREADY OVERCOME WITH EXHAUSTION, I leaned my head back on the seat as the plane took off. It was just the first leg of our journey back to the vast desert we had called home—a flight we'd been on many times before. After a few moments of unsuccessfully trying to sort my thoughts, I leaned forward to check on the kids sitting on either side of me. *What is going through their minds?* I wondered. This was so familiar yet so strange. It was the first time I would be on this flight back alone with my four children. Without Stephen.

It had been just over a year since Stephen's death. The question had never been *whether* we would return, but rather *when*. I felt the weight of loss like an anvil on my heart, yet it was mixed with indescribable joy and peace. Too many thoughts and emotions to sort through.

It was clear the children were sorting through some emotions of their own. Piper was the most excited, perhaps too young still to process the situation. They all were excited to go back to the familiar. To see their home, their friends, and the treasures we had left behind. But I knew that what we were going back to was going to be anything but familiar. Many of our belongings had been distributed and sold, and other people, strangers, now occupied our home. My heart sank deeper into an abyss as I tried to wrap my mind around the fact that we were not going back to Stephen. My heart ached for my kids, and I prayed earnestly for God's grace for them. I pushed my own grief aside. I had to be strong for them, but this would not be easy.

I had no idea what we would find when we landed. How would the locals react? Would they be glad we returned? Would they think we were crazy? Would the extremists be angry? Would we be easy targets for al-Qaeda?

At the suggestion of the regional security officer of the US embassy, we kept our arrival in the country secret even from our closest friends until we were on the ground. It was best not to be predictable. Several European aid workers had been kidnapped by al-Qaeda only a few months earlier.

Back home, many questioned the wisdom of our return, some out of concern for our safety and others out of resentment against Islam and the country where Stephen's life had been taken. Fear and anger had blurred the faith of several of our friends and family. They simply couldn't differentiate between Muslims who meant harm to us and the majority of the Muslims we called friends. "Our Muslim friends there had nothing to do with Stephen's death," I argued. I couldn't understand why they thought all Muslims were terrorists, and they couldn't understand why I didn't. I had to remind myself that their negative attitudes were based on their limited understanding of Islam. The ones who were most adamantly against our going back had never personally met a Muslim and certainly never had a real friendship with one. Returning was not easy, but fear was not among the plethora of emotions I was dealing with.

Once we landed, some dear friends came to pick us up. They had been working there for several years and were among the few American workers who'd decided to stay despite the incident and the unrest. It was a grand little reunion as our kids sat in the back of the SUV, giggling and talking. I was relieved to see some joy in my kids during this reentry.

As we drove through the city, my mind raced. The people were the same; the traffic was the same. Life simply carried on, as if nothing had happened.

Then the dreaded moment. The vehicle took a turn onto our street. As we drove slowly by our house, our life as we once knew it, my heart sank. As the kids and I gazed out the window I felt a tremendous pain in my heart, and my stomach began to ache. I wanted to speed away as quickly as possible. The kids just sat silently. I had no idea how to help them. I didn't know what to say to make it easier. I was at a complete loss. I fought the tears to no avail. I just turned my head the other direction and prayed for God to stop the pain.

Within a couple of hours it was as if the entire city knew we were home. My phone began to ring nonstop. So many friends wanted desperately to see us.

One of the most profound aspects of our return, one that I had not even considered, was the deep need our friends had to see us, to see that we were okay, to offer their condolences. So many had flocked to our house immediately after having received the news, and they had searched everywhere to make sure we were okay. They were also hurting. Their friend had been brutally murdered—and by men from their own country. Their friend's children were now fatherless, and his wife had been left a widow. They were battling their own emotions and heartache and longed to be there for us. And I deeply longed to be with them as well.

The next morning I started returning phone calls. Our first stop would be to our dear friends Amir and Jameila. The moment we pulled up outside, they ran out to greet us. Amir embraced each of us, and the children he embraced for a long time. Jameila wrapped her arms around me, sobbing. We both nearly fell to the ground.

During this visit, Amir recounted his experience in the rain the night Stephen was killed. "My brother has gone to be with our Lord, but we must carry on his legacy," he said fervently. "We must carry on with the work the Lord has given us to do."

He paused, then looked at me with a calmness and

boldness I had never seen before. "As you know," he continued, "I have always dealt with fear not only for my own life, but the lives of my wife and children. But I tell you, that fear is gone. Did you know that Stephen had come to see me only days before his death and sat right here in this room? He was very sick with fever, but he came anyway. I was concerned for his health. But he had an unusual sense of joy in his voice when he told me"—Amir's voice cracked—"'Amir, I don't know the number of my days. I could die tomorrow. Whether I die by illness or at the hands of extremists, life is too short. We must obey God while we still have breath in our bodies—before we no longer have a chance.'"

In visit after visit, with Muslims and believers alike, many tears were shed as they shared stories of things Stephen had said or done. Over and over, I was amazed at the amount of emotion being expressed by my Muslim friends.

Many locals whom I didn't know found where we were staying or got my phone number from someone in order to call to offer their condolences. "Your husband was a great man of God," they would say. "I have never met a Muslim who was as great a man as him." A wealthy businessman told me, "Our country has lost a great man."

One government official found where I was staying and came to pay me a visit. After I served him a cup of tea, he looked at me with anger in his eyes and said, "How can your family forgive those men who killed your husband? They are not Muslims. They are dogs who deserve to die." I was touched by his emotion for our family—and I had the opportunity to explain that we follow Jesus and that Jesus teaches us to love our enemies and bless those who persecute us. He was speechless.

So many people couldn't understand this. "But how can you forgive them?" "Why would you forgive them?" "How can you even return to this country that took your husband's life?" Forgiveness seemed to be a very foreign concept to them. They were genuinely astonished and confused. Stephen's death had a profound impact on these people— and our family's display of forgiveness is still talked about to this day.

We were surprised to discover that there was a rumor circulating that Stephen had recited the Muslim testimony of faith to become a Muslim just before he was shot. My first reaction was disdain, but then I realized that this was how many of Stephen's dearest Muslim friends were coping with his death. They were comforted by this rumor because they wanted to think that Stephen had accepted what they believed to be the truth before he died. They could not bear the thought of Stephen going to hell. I was deeply touched. And on many occasions I took the opportunity to set the story straight and explain that to follow Jesus Christ, the Way, the Truth, and the Life—the only way to God—meant that Stephen never had a doubt that to be absent from the body was to be present with the Lord (2 Corinthians 5:8).

Preparing to leave after our two-week visit was surreal. It didn't feel right that we were only visiting—it still felt like our home. As the plane took off, we all were plastered to the windows, looking over the vast desert terrain, refusing to say good-bye. As the tears fell, I felt the Lord speak to my heart once again: "The work is not done. I will continue to use you to water the seed." Pain and peace were in harmony. I will never understand how suffering and joy can coexist so beautifully.

A few weeks after Stephen's death, our US ambassador held a special memorial service for Stephen, planting an olive tree in the compound of the US embassy. Many local government officials attended. Stephen's father, James, asked for a monument to be erected at the place where Stephen's life was taken. He wanted the words "God Is Love" to be inscribed on the monument in English, French, and Arabic as a reminder that Stephen came to that country simply because he was compelled by God's love for its people. For many months the ambassador tried to make contact with the city mayor to have the monument authorized, but to no avail. James was persistent and hopeful; I was ready to give up.

The following year, the ambassador held another memorial service to mark the one-year anniversary of Stephen's death. Our family had the honor of being included through Skype. We were able to express to those present how much Stephen had loved his God and their country, and that our family's love and prayers for the country had not wavered in the face of our tragedy. We were later told that many of the government officials who were in attendance were in tears at our words. At the end of the service, the ambassador and the local minister of the interior unveiled a plaque by the olive tree that read, "In Memoriam of Stephen Foreman: 'A man of peace whose death shall overcome hate.'"

After a moment of silence, the city mayor spoke up. "I request that everyone here please follow me to the place where Stephen Foreman gave his life," he said. "I have something I would also like to unveil in his honor." They reached the stretch of street where Stephen had died, now crowded during the busiest time of the afternoon. Passersby joined the convoy to hear the mayor's speech. The mayor expressed again how much Stephen was loved and appreciated by him and by his entire country. Then, as a hush settled over the crowd, he unveiled a monument inscribed with the words "God Is Love" in English, French, and Arabic.

Stephen's death was not the end. The work goes on in this vast desert country. I go back often with my children and other partners in ministry with whom God has blessed us. Stephen's father also returns regularly and has taken the role as chairman of the board of directors for our NGO. He carries on Stephen's passion to see the love of Christ be expressed through our projects, and he continues building friendships and discipling those who have started following Jesus.

God never ceases to amaze me with his faithfulness to our family. After losing Stephen I assumed that I would live the rest of my life a widow. No one could ever replace

Stephen, and besides, what of my children and continuing ministry? It seemed impossible that there would be someone out there who would love and serve God passionately and love my children and the people of North Africa as much as I. However, God in his sovereignty knew there was someone far more wonderful than I could have dreamed. Lewis and I married three years after my loss of Stephen. He was a widower himself with two children, and he was also working with our ministry in the States. The merging of our families and our ministry to the unreached has been a beautiful and blessed process. Lewis and I now continue working in North Africa together. He is loved and respected by our North African friends and is a wonderful asset to our discipleship efforts. I am overwhelmed at the fruit that continues to grow.

Our NGO work continues under the directorship of our dear brother, Timothy. Along with him, two other men have chosen to help continue the work. One man is a brother in Christ; the other is a young devoted Muslim. Stephen hired Yusuf less than two years before his death. I never had the opportunity to get to know this young man, and neither Stephen nor I had ever met his family. But Stephen told me he was a man of peace.

Yusuf is from a wealthy upper-class family who have been very ashamed of his choice to work with our NGO in the prisons. Yusuf is an educated man and could easily find a higher-paying job, but he has committed his life to working with us and continuing Stephen's legacy.

From the time Stephen was killed, Yusuf dreamed of visiting

America. After two years of preparation, he was able to get his visa. We were thrilled to have him stay with us in our home. He wanted to see everything where Stephen had grown up, wondering what kind of environment could have produced such a selfless and godly man. "Above all," he explained, "it has been my dream to visit Stephen's grave. Muslims believe that if you visit the grave of your loved one, you can speak directly to them and God will allow them to hear you."

I was blown away. Even the best Muslim doesn't know for sure whether he will be granted entry into paradise, but Yusuf seemed to have no doubt that Stephen was with God. As Stephen's parents and I stood there with Yusuf at the grave, he began to speak to Stephen:

"Peace be upon you, my friend Stephen. I come here to express to you how much you mean to me and to my country. I want to express gratitude on behalf of all of the poor that you helped. You helped so many people. On behalf of my entire country and the 1,500 prisoners, I thank you for your willingness to come and live with us and help us. You helped so many. You did so much for—"

He buried his face in his hands and wept uncontrollably. Unable to speak, he just stood there and sobbed. Stephen's father walked over and put his arm around him and they both wept. Stephen's mother and I also stood weeping, trying to absorb what was taking place. After a moment, Yusuf regained enough composure to apologize, explaining that in his country and in his religion it is shameful for a man to cry like this in public.

"Yusuf," Stephen's mother said gently, "we believe that God gave us this emotion to express our feelings and our love for people. We see now that you did truly love our son. Thank you."

I've often been asked, "How is it that it was your family who suffered most in this tragedy, yet you continue to come back?"

The answer is easy. "I don't know the men who killed my husband," I tell them, "but I know you, and I know the people of this beloved country. And I love you, and more importantly, I serve a God who loves you passionately."

Yes, we will never get over the tragedy we faced. Stephen's death has left a lasting void in our hearts. The loss of a loved one is like an amputation. You will heal and you will learn to function and move on, but you will always have that void. I have experienced pain, but I have experienced healing. I've observed this same gentle healing in my kids' hearts. They miss their dad terribly, yet they are proud of him. They are proud to be his. Each of them has been through their own unique struggles in the healing process, but God has been faithful. We have experienced loss, but we are rich. As Jesus says in Mark 10:29-30,

> No one who has left home or brothers or sisters or mother or father or children or fields for me and the gospel will fail to receive a hundred times as much

in this present age: homes, brothers, sisters, mothers, children and fields—along with persecutions—and in the age to come eternal life.

We have many brothers and sisters and families and children that God has given us for our inheritance in North Africa. The richness of relationships that God has blessed us with are precious and too many to count.

God seems to be increasing my inheritance in the US as well. He continues to deepen my love for Muslims. Living and sharing life with Muslims for so many years in North Africa made it easy for me to connect with Muslims here in America. I've spent much time enjoying deep friendships with Muslim immigrants and refugees. These are friendships that transcend cultural and religious differences. My burden for them deepens as I witness the struggles they face trying to adapt to our culture and way of life. Having once been the guest in a host country, I can empathize with my dear Muslim friends who come here to the US as foreigners needing to learn a language and how to survive in a culture and way of life completely foreign to them. However, the difference between my experience as the foreigner and theirs is that when we were the foreigners in their land, trying to learn their language and way of life, they welcomed us with open arms. They understood that we were different in many ways, but most were excited to get to know us and to share their culture with us. Unfortunately, it isn't so for the majority of Muslim immigrants who come to America. Instead of hospitality, they find closed doors, walls, and in many cases disdain for the Muslim world. Instead of friends, so many find that Americans are afraid and suspicious of them.

"Why don't you just engage in conversation with Americans so that they know you are a peaceful and friendly person?" I asked my friend Miriam, an immigrant from Morocco. Her reply shamed me: "I know how Americans, especially here in the south, feel about Muslims and about my family. I know they don't want me here. I can handle the harsh glares and rude comments, but it hurts deeply to see my children experience it. In my culture, it is the honor of the host to extend hospitality, and not to do so would bring tremendous shame on an entire family." Miriam's husband even encouraged his teenage daughter not to wear the hijab so that people wouldn't think ill of her. But his daughter insisted on wearing it. She is proud of her culture, and she loves her heritage. My heart breaks for all of Miriam's family. They are some of the kindest, most peaceful, most compassionate people I know, and they sincerely love God. Here in America they may be the minority, but in the Muslim world, they are of the majority who long for peace.

The truth is, there are terrorists in the world who happen to be of the Muslim faith. There are even those who are moving to America as missionaries. There are extremists who are trying to change our way of life. How should we as true followers of Christ respond? Is shutting them out the answer? As Americans we naturally want to preserve our culture, our rights, and our freedom. But what if, in choosing the fear that we may lose our country, we actually lose our ability to be salt and light to a lost world? Is it worth it? Sometimes the pursuit of safety can be at odds with doing what is right. Is seeing God's Kingdom elevated above our own country worth the risk? I am American. I'm proud to be an American, but my loyalty lies first in my heavenly citizenship. When we died to ourselves, we died to anything that would stand in the way of our lives bringing honor to God among the nations.

As I ponder the struggle between faith and fear, I'm drawn back to a message that Stephen gave at a gathering in the US only a few days before returning to North Africa and giving his life only months later:

> When James Calvert went out as a missionary to the cannibals of the Fiji islands, the ship captain tried to turn him back, saying, "You'll lose your life and the lives of those with you if you go among those savages." To that Calvert replied, "We died before we came here." That's my question for us again tonight. Are you dead yet? Dead to yourself, dead to your own desires, dead to fear? Are we alive in Christ? My desire is that when people see your life, when they see my life, they will see Christ, and Christ alone. Let us live our lives as if they weren't our own lives. To truly be strangers in this world. To be aliens in this world. Our citizenship is in heaven.

Our citizenship is in heaven. Stephen lived those words, and died in those words—and lives in those words again. Although the loss of Stephen is one that will never leave us and has changed us completely, we hold on to the promise that God is glorified and that lives are being eternally changed because Stephen died before he stepped off that plane in the desert. And we have to continually answer the question that Stephen wrote shortly before his death: *Do we have something worth dying for, living for, moving for?*

To live without purpose is worse than dying.